BRINGING WOMEN INTO MANAGEMENT

BRINGING WOMEN INTO MANAGEMENT

Edited by
FRANCINE E. GORDON
Graduate School of Business
Stanford University

MYRA H. STROBER
Graduate School of Business
Stanford University

McGRAW-HILL BOOK COMPANY
New York   St. Louis   San Francisco   Auckland
Düsseldorf   Johannesburg   Kuala Lumpur   London
Mexico   Montreal   New Delhi   Panama   Paris
São Paulo   Singapore   Sydney   Tokyo   Toronto

Library of Congress Cataloging in Publication Data

Gordon, Francine E
  Bringing women into management.

  Based on a conference held Apr. 18, 1974 at the Stanford University Graduate
School of Business.
  Includes bibliographical references.
  1. Women executives—Addresses, essays, lectures. 2. Women—Em-
ployment—Addresses, essays, lectures. 3. Women—Legal status, laws,
etc.—Addresses, essays, lectures. I. Strober, Myra H., joint author. II.
Title.
HF5500.2.G67   658.4   75-1247
ISBN 0-07-023806-5
ISBN 0-07-023805-7 pbk.

BRINGING WOMEN INTO MANAGEMENT

1 2 3 4 5 6 7 8 9 0 M U M U 7 9 8 7 6 5

This book was set in Times Roman by Black Dot, Inc.
The editors were William J. Kane and Joseph F. Murphy;
the cover was designed by Rafael Hernandez;
the production supervisor was Judi Frey.
The Murray Printing Company was printer and binder.

Acknowledgments

The first quotation on page vi is from "The Road Not Taken" from *The Poetry of
Robert Frost* edited by Edward Connery Lathem. Copyright 1916, © 1969 by Holt,
Rinehart and Winston, Inc. Copyright 1944 by Robert Frost. Reprinted by
permission of Holt, Rinehart and Winston, Inc.

The second quotation on page vi is an untitled poem by Carol Diana Rudoff.
Copyright © 1975 by Carol Diana Rudoff and used with her permission.

To the men in our lives, Shelly and Sam

Two roads diverged in a wood, and I—
I took the one less traveled by,
And that has made all the difference.

—Robert Frost

Reflections of the past
To mirror what will be.
Each life can blend
And weave and bend—
Or wipe the mirror clean.

—Carol Diana Rudoff

Contents

List of Contributors

David L. Bradford
Lecturer in Organizational Behavior, Graduate School of
Business, Stanford University.

B.A., Oberlin College; Ph.D. (Social Psychology),
University of Michigan. Dr. Bradford, a specialist on
interpersonal processes within organizations, has been
concerned with the impact on white male managers of
employing women and minorities. He has been teaching a
course on women and minorities in organizations.

Cynthia Fuchs Epstein
Associate Professor of Sociology, Queens College of the
City University of New York.

B.A., Antioch College; M.A. (Sociology), New School for
Social Research; Ph.D. (Sociology), Columbia University.
A widely published author on the professional woman, Prof.
Epstein writes on the difficulties and pressures women

must face on the job and at home. Her publications include *Woman's Place*, a classic in the field of research on women, plus innumerable articles such as "Bringing Women In," "Women in Professional Life," and "Encountering the Male Establishment."

Francine E. Gordon
Assistant Professor of Organizational Behavior, Graduate School of Business, Stanford University.

B.A., Vassar College; M.A., Ph.D. (Administrative Sciences), Yale University. Professor Gordon teaches and conducts research on the effects on women of structures, attitudes, and interpersonal relations in organizations. Her present research is on women's psychological and physiological responses to job stress. She is coauthor of "The Career Choices of Married Women" and "Self-Image and Stereotypes of Femininity: Their Relationship to Women's Role Conflicts and Coping." Professor Gordon was one of the coorganizers of the Stanford Women in Management Conference.

Carol Nagy Jacklin
Research Associate, Department of Psychology, Stanford University.

B.A., M.A. (Experimental Psychology), University of Connecticut; Ph.D. (Experimental Child Psychology), Brown University. Dr. Jacklin has been studying the development of sex differences. Her most recent research is a longitudinal study of sex differences from birth to first grade. She has coauthored several articles including "Sex Differences in Intellectual Functioning," "Sex Role Stereotyping in the Public Schools," and "Stress, Activity and Proximity Seeking: Sex Differences in the Year Old Child." Dr. Jacklin has just coauthored a book with Eleanor Maccoby entitled *The Psychology of Sex Differences*, destined to be the definitive reference on the subject.

Eleanor Emmons Maccoby
Professor of Psychology, Stanford University.

B.S., University of Washington; M.A., Ph.D. (Psychology), University of Michigan. A renowned developmental

psychologist, Professor Maccoby has done extensive
research on the development of sex differences. Her long
list of publications includes *The Development of Sex
Differences*, a multiauthored book which has been the
authoritative work in the field. Her most recent writing,
The Psychology of Sex Differences, coauthored with Carol
Nagy Jacklin, is a new landmark. Other coauthored
publications include "Parents' Differential Reactions to
Sons and Daughters," "Attachment and Dependency,"
and *Patterns of Child Rearing*.

Colquitt L. Meacham
Teaching Fellow, School of Law, Harvard University.

B.A., Salem College; LL.B., Emory University. Ms.
Meacham has taught several courses on women in
law and society. In addition to writing "Sex Discrimination
in Government Benefits" and "Discrimination: Race and
Sex," she organized and conducted a seminar on
marriage and divorce laws that was filmed by CBS News
for "Sixty Minutes." In 1972, Ms. Meacham was voted
outstanding young woman of the year for California.

Arjay Miller
Professor of Management and Dean, Graduate School of
Business, Stanford University.

B.S., LL.D. (Hon.), University of California at Los Angeles;
LL.D. (Hon.), Whitman College; LL.D. (Hon.), University of
Nebraska. Dean Miller is a leading member of the
business community. Prior to his coming to Stanford, he
was President of the Ford Motor Company and Chairman
of the Automobile Manufacturers Association. In addition
to his Business School responsibilities, Dean Miller is
presently on the Board of Directors of the Ford Motor
Company, Levi Strauss and Company, Utah International
Incorporated, The Washington Post Company, and Wells
Fargo Bank, and he is on the Board of Trustees of the
Brookings Institution, The Conference Board, and the
Urban Institute. As an educator and as an executive, he is
aware of the importance of increasing the number of
women in upper levels of management. Dean Miller was a
key figure in bringing about the Stanford Women in
Management Conference.

Alice G. Sargent
Consultant to NTL Institute for the Development of Sex
Roles Program.

B.A., Oberlin College; M.A. (English Literature), Brandeis
University; Ed.D. (Human Relations), School of Education,
University of Massachusetts. In addition to her activities at
the NTL Institute, Dr. Sargent does extensive consulting
for private industry and for local, state, and the federal
governments, organizing training programs to help
women in management. She is author of *Beyond Sex
Roles*, a handbook designed to facilitate change in sex
roles. Dr. Sargent is presently an associate editor of the
Journal of Applied Behavioral Science.

Melinda S. Sprague
Director of the Counseling Center, San Diego State
University.

B.A., Duke University; M.A. (Organizational Behavior),
Case Western Reserve; Ph.D. (Counseling and
Organizational Change), United States International
University. Dr. Sprague consults with organizations,
establishing affirmative action and training programs for
women in management.

Myra H. Strober
Assistant Professor of Economics, Graduate School of
Business, Stanford University.

B.S., Cornell University; M.A. (Economics), Tufts
University; Ph.D. (Economics), Massachusetts Institute of
Technology. Prof. Strober, a labor economist, teaches and
writes about the economic causes and effects of women's
increasing participation in the work world. She is the
author of "Discrimination: A Case of Lower Earnings for
Women, Comment" and "Formal Extrafamily Child Care:
Some Economic Observations." Prof. Strober is currently
writing a book, *Women in the American Economy*,
synthesizing and extending the vast amount of recent
research in this field. She was one of the coorganizers of
the Stanford Women in Management Conference.

Preface

On April 18, 1974, the Stanford Graduate School of Business sponsored a conference for executives on the topic, "Women in Management." This book is a direct outgrowth of that conference. The conference, the first of its kind in content and audience, was extremely successful. Our thanks are due to several persons: Samuel (Pete) Pond, Associate Dean and Director of Continuing Education, for providing initial support; Robert W. Simon, Assistant Dean for Corporate Relations, and Marion R. Rodenberger, Administrative Assistant, for their assistance with detailed planning; and Arjay Miller, Dean, for his advice and personal support. For additional assistance we'd like to acknowledge the Advisory Council of the Graduate School of Business (especially Richard P. Cooley, Chairman of the Advisory Council), G. L. Bach, Herbert A. Blanchett, Karen H. Campbell, Ann Hammer, F. E. Hunt, Mary Lanigar, Diane Duerr Levine, Anne S. Miner, Barney Olmsted, Jennifer Renzel, Mary L. Vivanco, Julia Walsh, and Sharon Weiner.

And now for the book. A special note of appreciation to E. Kirby Warren, Professor of Management at Columbia University, who encouraged us to contact various publishers. We further wish to thank Carol Greenwald and B. Jennine Anderson for permission to quote them, and to thank Carol Diana Rudoff, Carol Jacklin, and Eleanor Maccoby for permission to use their materials. Our thanks to Ruth Franklin for her editorial work on the manuscript. Her willingness to meet the most unrealistic deadlines contributed greatly to the completion of this book. And we appreciate the efforts of Carol Westermann and Marge Holford, two of the fastest typists in the West. Without the help of these and several unnamed people this book could never have been.

Francine E. Gordon
Myra H. Strober

BRINGING WOMEN INTO MANAGEMENT

Introduction
Arjay Miller

During my five years as dean of the Stanford Graduate School of Business, I have been urged to host numerous top-management conferences. Because I know how busy corporation executives are, however, it was not until the idea of such a conference on women in management arose that I acquiesced. Here was a subject of increasing significance and concern to all, and an area in which a properly structured program could help companies achieve the goal of increasing the number of women executives and maximizing their effectiveness. With this in mind, the Stanford Business School sponsored a conference in April 1974 on women in management. Business leaders from across the country attended. The success of the conference suggested that the presentations be developed into a book for permanent availability and wider distribution.

In the postwar period, the percentage of women in the labor force has grown rapidly. According to the 1970 census, 40 percent of the labor force is now female. Less than 20 percent of all management positions are held by women; however, precious few of these posts are the kind that would interest many M.B.A.'s. While about 11 percent of all males in the labor force are managers or administrators, less than 4 percent of all women in the labor force hold such positions. We all need to be concerned about why these percentages are so low, so that we do not squander the talents of the increasing numbers of women who are entering the schools of business and the business world.

As several of the chapters in this book indicate, the scarcity of women managers is due largely to the inertia caused by tradition. Most male managers have little interest in changing the situation and are often uncomfortable in dealing with female managers. At the same time, female managers have feelings of self-doubt, feelings generated by previous socialization experiences. Moreover, the formal and informal structures of large organizations often seem inflexible and hostile, and those who wish to initiate change aren't sure how to go about it.

Until recently, few voices were raised in protest over the inequities of the present situation; few women had expressed an interest in administrative careers and few organizations realized the waste of scarce abilities. Times have changed. An increased supply of potential women managers arises from new home and family life-styles growing out of new attitudes and aspirations on the part of women. Simultaneously, growing recognition that management talent is our scarcest resource has brought about an increasing demand for women managers.

Accelerating the transition, and giving it a persuasive urgency, has been the force of law. Most companies are subject to surveillance by the Equal Employment Opportunity Commission, the Office of Federal Contract Compliance, and, in some instances, state agencies and special watchdog divisions within the Department of Labor. The threat of court action has produced situations like the $30 million settlement in which the American Telephone and Telegraph Company agreed to compensate employees who, it was charged, suffered damage due to sex discrimination. As another example, a tire maker has agreed to add another 260 women to its management ranks by 1979, settling a bias charge brought by a former trainee. One harried corporate executive, chided by his peers for consenting in a sex bias action, was quick to retort, "Wait your turn. If they can do it to me, they can do it to you."

Another factor increasing the demand for women managers is the growing belief in the importance of interpersonal skills. Women are thought more likely to be interpersonally aware than men, not innately, but because they have been socialized into being so. It is hoped that these women will help discover new styles of management, enlarging the inventory of managerial skills for men as well as women.

In light of these trends, I am increasingly optimistic that supply and demand will grow apace, making for a lively market for female managers for years to come. The challenge will then become even more imperative: how to place more women in the topmost ranks of the corporate hierarchy.

Very few of today's top women executives are professionally trained managers. Rather, they have gained positions of influence through either an accident of birth (by being born into a family possessed of corporate wealth) or an act of marriage (leading to a widow's takeover). For these women, family ties were the only available routes to the top.

But women are no longer willing to rely solely on kinship or affectional ties to provide career advancement. The former trickle of applications from women for admission to the nationally recognized schools of business has become a deluge, and management-oriented courses at every level of higher education are becoming increasingly popular with women. To augment and diversify the ranks of the top-level women executives is the aspiration of today's new breed of professional women managers.

Quests for high-potential women managers should by all means include—but by no means be limited to—the better schools of management. Promising candidates may be found already hard at work within the corporate structure, and ample evidence of female ability in the management realm is to be found outside of the classroom or the corporate boardroom. Some of the most capable and dedicated women managers are doing volunteer work for churches, hospitals, and a variety of other nonprofit social and political groups. Once these women are identified, they should have access to a host of management development courses to aid their climb to the top. For such women, the traditional promotional practices will no longer be satisfactory. The authors of this book will be as disappointed as its readers if the book serves merely to increase the numbers of women stagnating in lower- and middle-management positions.

If women of high managerial aptitude are to reach their destinies—at once fulfilling society's needs and their own—they will have to be given the chance to perform at much higher levels than is now typical for women. I firmly believe women will live up to high expectations because of the past successes of those who have "accidentally" landed in top jobs despite the lack of professional training or on-the-job experience normally available to men. How much better women should perform with these handicaps removed and opportunities made truly equal.

The opening chapters of this book discuss organizational procedures and current attitudes toward women that have perpetuated their exclusion from the top ranks of corporate management. In Chapter I, Professor Epstein analyzes the institutional barriers which keep women from achieving top-management positions. In Chapters II and III, chapters not included in the Stanford Women in Management Conference, but written especially for this book, Dr. Carol Jacklin and Professor Eleanor Maccoby examine the influences of biology on women's capabilities and Drs. David Bradford, Alice Sargent, and Melissa Sprague look at the issues of sexuality as they relate to women in management.

As noted earlier, legal decisions regarding the employment of women have had a considerable impact on corporate obligations and attitudes. In Chapter IV, Colquitt Meacham presents an analysis of the impact of court decisions and administrative guidelines, and discusses likely future trends in areas of current uncertainty.

In Chapter V, Professor Myra Strober considers basic strategies designed to bring women into top management. Some of the strategies are of immediate benefit to the organization itself in terms of meeting short-term requirements; others yield more indirect and long-range benefits to a given organization while also meeting broad social goals.

Following Professor Strober's chapter is a case study of women in management. "Perfectly Pure Peabody's" is based on a real-life situation and provides readers with an opportunity to analyze the difficulties inherent in the implementation of an affirmative action program for women.

In Chapter VII, Professor Francine Gordon reviews the key factors which are required in a successful affirmative action program. Emphasis is on the specific role of the senior executive in creating the appropriate atmosphere and apparatus.

From Professor Gordon's analysis, the book moves to a chapter containing a series of individual vignettes. These present a concrete picture of the kinds of women discussed earlier—women now in business school, those displaying managerial talents in noncorporate settings, and those who are presently in corporate management. These are real persons, talking about who they are and where they are going.

In the final chapter of the book the editors comment on some of the vignettes of women in management and then explore the likely impact of this "new breed of manager" on organizations.

This book is intended to encourage and assist top management in bringing more women into management at all levels, particularly the upper echelons of the corporate world. It provides an intellectual understanding of the issues and practical information on how to implement change. Men and women alike will find this an exceedingly useful and enlightening volume.

Chapter I

Institutional Barriers: What Keeps Women Out of the Executive Suite?

Cynthia Fuchs Epstein

A movie of some years ago called *Barbarella* had a haunting scene in which the heroine, marooned in a wasteland, sees in the distance a horde of automated dolls, lovely, wide-eyed, long-haired dolls, the kind little girls have long cherished. But as Barbarella moves close to these creatures, she is dismayed and terrified to see that their mouths open and shut like those of puppets, emitting shrill sounds and revealing teeth that are steel traps, sharp and pointed.

This to me seems to symbolize current reality. Whether women ask for equality softly or firmly, the male gatekeepers, and some established women as well, often hear only shrill and piercing sounds. Requests are heard as demands. Demands seem to imply violence. This response is by no means universal but it predominates. It prolongs the resistance to women's participation in spheres long dominated by men, and reflects the continued cultural conflict between the norms specifying womanly or ladylike behavior and the norms specifying competent business and professional behavior.

Both our perceptions of behavior and our expectations as to proper behavior shape present conditions. Women newcomers to business and the professions still face age-old prejudices and cultural biases that define their roles and their potential contributions. These stereotypes intrude on their social and business relations with men and make assimilation difficult.[1]

Of primary importance are those informal structures of interaction in the business and professional world that affect and are affected by women's behavior. Informal behavior is institutionalized at least as thoroughly as the formal modes of interaction depicted on organizational charts, and it is probably more important to analyze informal interaction. The closer one gets to the top, the more commonly are decision-making judgments and rewards determined by subjective criteria; "understandings" rather than rules govern behavior, and personal qualifications are judged against a range of attributes not immediately relevant functionally to the job at hand. These factors have always been important, but they may become even more important as legal strictures forbid the exclusion of women and others once rejected categorically.

A. TRENDS IN THE STATUS OF WOMEN

Before considering the informal modes of institutional exclusion of women, we may review women's position, cross-culturally over the years, as it bears on these issues.

Perhaps the factor that best determines what may be women's work is not the nature of the work performed nor the burden it may create mentally or physically, but rather the symbolic significance of the work and whether or not it is considered important, honorable, and desirable. The greater the social desirability of a type of work, the less likely it is that women are identified with it. All societies seem to prefer *men* in the jobs most valued. Even where women constitute a majority among personnel of an occupation, such as in schoolteaching, librarianship, or textile work, men seem to have a disproportionately greater chance to be in the top administration of the field. This is true even in Soviet medicine, where men, although a minority of the profession, hold the top professorships and hospital administration posts.[2] In all cultures, women are at best tolerated in the most desired fields, and the few found there are regarded as having special and idiosyncratic traits that justify the anomaly.[3] This rationalizing impedes women's integration into top jobs even when few formal obstacles exist.

Although today we assume widespread changes in the position of women, there have probably been fewer significant changes than media publicity indicates. The 1970 census showed percentage increases for women in male-dominated professions and occupations not unlike those of the previous two decades. Women lawyers rose from 2.4 percent of the profession in 1940 to 3.5 percent in 1960 and 4.9 percent in 1970, a minimal increase in light of the enormous emphasis on women's liberation during the sixties. In medicine women moved from 6.5 percent of their profession in 1960 to 9.3 percent in 1970, but women were only 8.5 percent of all medical students that same year.[4] Presumably those percentages have increased since the 1970 census.

But some of the statistics point the other way. In manufacturing industries the percentage of managers dropped from 7.1 percent women in 1960 to 6.3 percent in 1970.[5] This was below the 6.4 percent listed in 1950, when the status of women was relatively lower than during the previous two decades and when the proportion of women dropped in all career-oriented spheres of life. It was a period characterized by Jessie Bernard as the time of the "motherhood mania."

There are few reliable statistics about women's opportunities for promotion in publishing, banking, commerce, or the public utilities. When the statistics are at hand, it will then be necessary to look beyond the new titles to the actual roles being filled.[6] Visibility is a central problem for women in business and the other male-dominated professional activities. Certain jobs are less visible than others, and those in the former don't get as much credit as they would otherwise. Women tend to get the jobs that are actually and symbolically less visible—*actually*, because they do not have contact with clients and with the market, and *symbolically*, because the jobs they have are not defined as crucial.

One further complication is that even where women are given higher-level administrative jobs, these do not lead to top-management posts, but rather are on ancillary routes that may be dead ends. A woman may be called a vice president or special assistant to the president, but be assigned to administrate an affirmative action plan or asked to recruit women personnel. Such activity is rarely viewed as more than peripheral to the goals of the firm and is unlikely to lead to the top. Today the diverging of women to alternative routes may occur at a higher level than before, but the ultimate consequences are the same.

1. Characteristics of Women in Top Management

There are still so few women executives that certain tantalizing questions must go unanswered: e.g., Are there "self-made" women in the same sense that some men are seen as self-made? A study attempted by the Harvard Business School in the late sixties had to be abandoned for lack of sufficient subjects. In 1966 the British Political and Economic Planning organization (PEP) sponsored a study of women in managerial jobs in government service, the British Broadcasting Corporation, and two large companies. The team of researchers, headed by Michael Fogarty and Rhona and Robert Rapoport, reported on their work in two volumes published in 1971 called *Women in Top Jobs* and *Sex, Career and Family*.[7] They found that women who rose to the top of these organizations did so largely because of chance, the wartime diversion of manpower, or the death of a relative. It was clear that the women who assumed directorship roles under these conditions would not have sought them, nor been offered them, under normal circumstances.

In the United States in 1971 Margaret Hennig[8] studied twenty-five women presidents and vice presidents of medium-to-large nationally recognized business firms, out of the one hundred women who then held such posts. Most were widows or daughters of men who had led these firms or women who had other ties with a man in command. *Fortune*, in an article on the ten top-paid women in the United States, reported a similar situation that serves to underline the importance of affectional or kinship ties in determining women's success.[9]

Why should this be so? In a world where the door is barred to women, only a few get in totally uninvited, most of them because of special circumstances. Friendship and kinship provide an alternative opportunity structure, paralleling a system of protégéship by which men gain entrance to the inner circles. As intimates of the mighty, women have access to the information *any* aspirant needs to mount the ladder of success. But the route of marriage or friendship has never been a true alternative opportunity structure. It is a testament to the subtle skills of the gatekeepers that the underlying disapproval elicited by this kind of alternative route serves as a social control mechanism to ensure that women, already denied recourse to the male strategem, cannot truly succeed by the only strategem open to them.[10]

For women, the costs of using a particularistic route are high and the profits are always contingent. Positions won by being tied to one man are nontransferable. Until a woman has proven herself, she is in a poor bargaining position for title or money. Her competence is always under scrutiny, and many women can prove their talent only after the death of a husband, if they succeed to his position.

2. Mechanisms of Exclusion

Not only is competition keen for the pinnacles, but active mechanisms thin the ranks of the competitors. Women, like other groups who have potential talent and ability, have been kept out of the pool of eligibles in science, law, and other male-dominated professions. A certain evenness of resistance to the inclusion of women is apparent in these spheres long dominated by men. Women have not had access to the same reward structure that men have, and this is as much a cause of their low participation and productivity in the professions as is the discrimination that bars them.[11]

In some ways the exclusion of women may have been more effective than the barring of other groups because women, unlike the other groups, have had an initial acculturation to values of the ruling elites. They have grown up with men, learned their manners, been educated in their schools, and been exposed to the same circuitry of contacts. But the Radcliffe sisters of Harvard brothers and their other Ivy League counterparts, classes of 1940, 1950, and 1960 (which produced the heads of our corporations, the rulers of our country), somehow were tracked into careers, not usually called careers, as adjuncts to their husbands.

Careers in corporate and government life have typically been so demanding that men have needed able wives to entertain, soothe, make contacts, and offer ballast. Most top careers, in fact, have been cooperative efforts, but husbands hold the titles and power and their wives serve as statusless, unpaid partners.[12] As corporations institutionalized the twelve-hour day for their executives and developed a set of expectations that a man's family be at the call of the corporation, both the single man and the man whose wife who has an independent life have been hampered in the climb to power. The woman executive is likewise handicapped. Given the norms of family life in America, she could hardly be expected to make the same demands on her husband that the husband can make on his wife.

When it was inconceivable for women to be on the same path as men, alternative routes to the top were suggested. As secretaries or gal Fridays, serving men, supposedly they would learn the ropes. Actually some did, and realized too late that it was not know-how alone that would give them promotions; it was knowledge acquired in specified settings and according to certain rules. Women who insisted they be given the same chances as men were seen as immodest and pushy, lacking in the very qualities of charm and grace that made women nice to have around. The female recruit entered the world of work with a built-in bias, with a different set of experiences, without a peer group, to face a situation where she would be damned if she did and damned if she didn't perform well. The British study of women directors indicated that colleagues saw them as "dragons" if they were authoritative, or as "nice mice" if they were mild in demeanor.

3. Problems of Identification

Some of the structures within the occupations are becoming more clearly recognized today as being instrumental in making women feel uncomfortable and unwanted.

The business world has for a long time considered women executives to be such a rarity that clients and colleagues could only react with surprise or disbelief. Most men assumed that any woman at a business meeting was a secretary. A woman executive often had to announce who she was, had no implicit status, and had difficulty exerting authority. Imagine a male executive who could *always* expect to be mistaken for the salesman or the filing clerk, and would have to identify himself and hope he would be treated with respect. Men in positions of authority expect that others will know their power. In fact, they know that the more power they have, the less they need to announce it. Lesser men can lean on the image of power, emulating the model member of upper corporation management in classic gray flannel suit with vest, and assume an air of detached authority. For women there has been no comparable model.

Ironically, as types of authority loosen and the male executive tends to be more approachable and informal, women may face greater ambiguity in defining their roles than before. One may call the boss "Bill" rather than "Mr. Jones" and still not upset the power structure, because it is clear who stands in authority. But calling the boss "Jane" rather than "Ms. Hastings" may easily produce a patronizing and comradely ambience in which lines of power, difficult to read swiftly between men and women in the clearest of circumstances, are misunderstood.

B. CONSEQUENCES OF THE NUMBERS OF WOMEN IN TOP POSITIONS

We must also consider the relevance of numbers and ratios in interaction. When women in management are few in number, they feel excluded and often become estranged. They say they are not really considered to be part of the organization in a true membership sense, but interlopers. Women's minority position in management is institutionalized by rules guaranteeing a tiny quota. When there is only one woman in the executive suite, it is awkward for her; she has no peer group, no referent for her behavior.[13] And it is awkward for her male colleagues, who perceive her as a lone intruder to their all-male bastion. It is essential to create a critical mass in management, a large enough proportion of women to make their presence a matter of course rather than a phenomenon.

1. Informal Interaction

Numbers and ratios are significant in establishing the all-important norms of informal social interaction, a process that is of utmost importance in top-management circles. Consider the key informal contacts made over lunch, or the easy camaraderie of the bar. A male colleague might feel awkward asking a woman business associate to have a drink, and vice versa. One man to one woman suggests an overture to a specifically social relationship, and the combination of three men and one woman may seem awkward to the woman who might feel like an intruder on their "man talk"; but if there were four men and two women, or three men, then the informal social relations intertwined with business would not have a sexual overtone. In other contexts where no arbitrary rules limit the normal exchanges between men and women, work proceeds smoothly. The mere presence of women does not disrupt the structure, and the men don't feel diminished.

The consequences of a social pattern that distinguishes between men and women in terms of membership, dining rooms, dining tables, or mere access may be more injurious then the degradation suffered by those who are wholly excluded. When women cannot mingle easily with men as colleagues in the informal settings where business gets done, they cannot become fully prepared to exercise influence. When women expect and are given full participation in the formal and informal structures of their occupations at every level, including the top one, they can be included as equals and be let in on the silent rules of the game along with the males.

2. The Reward-Punishment System

With this model of membership a woman would be prepared to make a contribution on her own. She would have to become, as they say, her own "man." She would have to know that her performance will face the same tests as those of men and that on the same criteria she will succeed or fail. This model would not shelter or hide women in invisible positions. It would convince them that if they contribute, they will rise in rank and increase in visibility and be paid and respected accordingly; if they fail, it is not because they are women but because their performance has been found wanting. And as they rise, the standards will become higher, as with men. When men are clearly at the top, the driving motivation for them ceases to be the expectation of greater rewards—more money or even more rank—but the need (gradually internalized over time) to *continue to achieve.* Few women have so far been exposed to this conditioning.

3. Processes in the Creation of Criteria for Competence

We are concerned about the way in which business roles are institutionalized so that only *certain* people are seen as appropriate partners in normal interaction. Denial of access to the structure in which competence is created has perpetuated the exclusion of women from top posts. Those who are not admitted or who are not *admissible* to inner circles are denied what is perhaps the most crucial learning of their trade. This is most obvious in the case of professions. Top surgeons learn their special skills not when they are in medical school, but when they are selected to be residents with the finest physicians in their specialty. Top lawyers start as apprentices to the senior partners in the large firms. The process is comparable in business, where most skills are not objectively learned but are rather the product of intelligence, diplomacy, know-how, and "know-who." Information about who is the best producer of an item and what kind of pricing is possible is passed on to protégés, who are also introduced to top people.

Our social conditioning encourages us to think of persons of only a certain age or sex or race as being able to understand tasks or to carry them out. Women have not been thought of as business executives, and younger men too have often been discriminated against, simply because they seemed too young to hold a job of responsibility and did not fit the mold. Discrimination is not always directed at the *classic* underdog, but it works against any group that does not fit the stereotype. We may not pity the young man because we expect he will *ultimately* get the position for which he might be fit now. We think he is too young partially because we know that older people do not like to be commanded by the young. But he is also handicapped by our stereotypes about how many years a person should devote to each stage of his career. These expectations are defined by how it has always been done. We also have views about the amount of time any particular task ought to take and how long the workday ought to be for a "committed" person. On all sides we are encumbered by expectations that are operationalized as coercive rules. They are rationalized as logical, but a closer look shows that they are based on unchallenged assumptions and reflect the status quo. These assumptions typically favor the class of persons in command and make others seem to be the "wrong" persons for the job, whoever they are and whatever the job may be.

4. Style, Self, and the Aura of Competence

We must be concerned about the difficulty of objective evaluation of competence. Psychological and sociological studies make clear the impact of "labeling," the process by which a person is called competent or incompetent, appropriate or inappropriate, good or bad. The label defines the self-image that in turn shapes the behavior. A person who is seen as a "go-getter" likely to succeed will work harder than the person who is perceived as inept and unable to accomplish a goal or a dream.

The more we study people who are ostensibly "self-made," the more we see that what really made them is not only their idiosyncratic set of talents but also the framework in which they lived, the opportunities available to them, and the role of persons important in their lives in the formation of a self-image that facilitated career attainments.

Gatekeepers are often so committed to stereotypes that they are incapable of seeing talent or emerging competence because the package in which it is presented is so unexpected. If we do not listen to the brilliant woman because we don't expect bright ideas to come in a female form, we won't hear her contribution. And when, after a while, she falls silent because no one listens, the initial stereotype is confirmed and reinforced.[14] There are, of course, exceptions to this pattern, but again our stereotypes get in the way.

Women in politics say that because Bella ⟨
and forthright in her personal style, her congres
find it embarrassing to interact with her and they ⟨
as much as possible. It is clear that many male polit.   ⌐me
an aggressive personal style that is not only tolerated   ⌐ defined
as consistent with leadership. The woman, however, is caught in a
morass of conflicting expectations and may be damned whatever
style she chooses.

An increase in the numbers of women in male settings will
doubtless change current attitudes that accept a greater range of
styles for men than for women. Then any one woman's personal
style would be less attributable to all women, and each would be
accepted as an individual, as is any man. Enough women would
be visible at one time to make clear the lack of homogeneity. This
has already been demonstrated to some degree in formerly male
bastions, such as business and law schools, that now admit
substantial percentages of women students. Male students and
teachers are accepting women and judging them according to
the same standards as men. Men in business and professions do
not necessarily intend to discriminate. We all tend to define what
we see most often as normal. The world in which they work is
mostly male, and that is the most comfortable and natural way for
them. Probably few are even aware that women are excluded or
made to feel unwanted, although in certain cases the possibility of
bad intentions cannot be ignored.

Exclusionary consequences can flow from good motives as
well as bad. Some men really do think they are helping a woman
by being sensitive to her family responsibilities and not asking her
to do the extra work that might be just what she needs to prove
her talents and perhaps get a promotion. This paternalism deprives women of the right to decide independently and thereby to
learn. No single answer will fit all women, and each must choose
her own priorities in life and be free to act accordingly.

5. Culture and the Structure of Motivation

What is unique about the situation of women today is that almost
everyone is to blame, including women themselves, who have
joined the conspiracy by accepting the idea that they must
monitor their ambitions and goals in terms of what everybody

se expects of them—including their husbands, children, fathers, or bosses. Our culture expects and encourages women to hold back, not to "go for broke": not to sacrifice family savings or the immediate comfort of the family in service of long-range goals. But this is exactly what is expected of a man who is an entrepreneur or struggling professional. Clearly, motivational structures are not alike for men and women.[15]

While both his private and professional lives combine to encourage the man to put his best into his work and promise him rewards for doing so, the woman's private life—the home and community—tends to undermine her work goals, presenting challenges to her right to work and outright hostility. Community values will often condemn her career goals as antisocial and an abandonment of husband and children. In her professional life, her colleagues often question her ability and the extent and depth of her commitment. On the basis of an incomplete assessment of her own accomplishments she may form a negative self-image that she then extends, somewhat defensively, to characterize women more generally. These women often stifle their desire for self-fulfillment or deflect it in other directions, some of them destructive to the husbands and children through whom they try to live vicariously.

C. CHANGE AND RESISTANCE TO CHANGE IN THE STATUS OF WOMEN

Things can change, and there is evidence that they are changing. My findings[16] in studying women in elite positions in business and the professions show that the old homily "Nothing succeeds like success" is well grounded in fact. It is a self-fulfilling prophecy not unlike the labeling discussed above. Yet I believe that the idea of opening the doors to women somehow, whether for traditional, cultural, or psychological reasons, seems a basic threat that will always stand in the way of truly equal opportunities in management for both sexes.

These fears are not groundless; they stem from women's obvious potential. It is certainly true that women, who constitute such a large proportion of the educated, could take over quite a few men's jobs tomorrow if they were so inclined and if they were given the opportunity. Yet it must be possible to devise work structures in which we can upgrade *all* jobs, provide reward incentives for all, and define competition from the bottom to the top in terms of sheer creative talent, ambition, and drive.

The search continues for specific structural solutions to these problems. These cannot succeed without a simultaneous concern with the attitudes that are created early in life in the home and in school, for changing attitudes and changing structure go hand in hand. We may change work conditions more easily than attitudes, but no situation is hopeless. The large law firms that have employed women and have even made them senior partners find that clients accept the judgment of the firm as to who will serve them well. Further, no firm has reported suffering a financial loss or a diminution of prestige for doing so.

At General Motors, once directives were handed down from top management to expedite the affirmative action program demanded by the government, GM's middle managers not only went along, but often found good reasons for changing the old practices. Everyone, it seems, became interested in the success of the plan.

The American Telephone and Telegraph Company now has a vice president who is mobilizing a task force of bright managers to rethink job sequences, job criteria, and job segmentation. They are going beyond the thinking lodged in commonplace notions about how things have been done. Of course, such innovations will have many consequences beyond simply assimilating women.

Women have generally been deprived of the charisma of the halo effect of title and rank. When officers of business concerns give women the same deference as well as accoutrements of office given men, women will be more at ease in assuming command. When firms back women executives with the expectations that they will do well and let their subordinates know it, women will measure up to these expectations. But the institution must feel it has a stake in the person and vice versa. Job commitment and high performance cannot develop when women sense that the promises held out to them are empty, or tokens intended primarily to pacify the demands of EEOC. Women have long permitted themselves to accept a bad bargain, but today more and more they are insisting on a fair price, the market price, for their services.

NOTES

I would like to acknowledge the invisible structure of the reasoning in this paper which, in part, relies on a number of concepts developed by Robert K. Merton in *Social Theory and Social Structure* (Chicago, Ill.: Free Press, 1957). Among those which I immediately identify are those of the power of relative and absolute numbers in the dynamics of social groups; the emergence of a notion of deviance on the part of those whose status sets are inconsistent with the pattern most frequently seen; the unintended consequences of intent; and the self-fulfilling prophecy. Similarly, I am indebted to the perspective offered by Erving Goffman on the presentation of the self.

1 Lawrence C. Hackamack and Alan B. Solid, "The Woman Executive: There Is Still Ample Room for Progress," *Business Horizons*, April 1972, pp. 89–93; and Benson Rosen and Thomas H. Jerdee, "Sex Stereotyping in the Executive Suite," *Harvard Business Review*, March–April 1973, pp. 45–58.

2 Norton T. Dodge, *Women in the Soviet Economy*, Baltimore: Johns Hopkins, 1966.

3 Eleanor Brantley Schwartz, "The Sex Barrier in Business," *Atlanta Economic Review*, June 1971, p. 6.

4 "The Economic Role of Women," *Economic Report of the President*, Washington, D.C., 1973.

5 Ibid., p. 101.

6 Burton G. Malkiel and Judith A. Malkiel, "Male-Female Pay Differentials in Professional Employment," *American Economic Review*, September 1973, pp. 693–705.

7 Michael Fogarty, Rhona Rapoport, and Robert Rapoport, *Women in Top Jobs: Four Studies in Achievement* and *Sex, Career and Family*, prepared jointly by Political and Economic Planning (PEP) and the Tavistock Institute, London: G. Allen, 1971.

8 Margaret Marie Hennig, "Career Development for Women Executives," unpublished doctoral dissertation, Harvard University, Cambridge, Mass., 1971.

9 Wyndham Robertson, "Ten Highest Ranking Women in Big Business," *Fortune*, April 1973, pp. 80–89.

10 Cynthia Fuchs Epstein, "Bringing Women In: Rewards, Punishments, and the Structure of Achievement," *Annals of the New York Academy of Sciences*, March 1973, pp. 62–70.

11 Cynthia Fuchs Epstein, "Structuring Success for Women: Guidelines for Gatekeepers," *Journal of the National Association of Women Deans and Counselors*, Fall 1973, pp. 34–42.

12 Cynthia Fuchs Epstein, "Law Partners and Marital Partners: Strains and Solutions in the Dual-Career Family Enterprise," *Human Relations*, December 1971, pp. 549–564.

13 Eleanor Brantley Schwartz and James J. Rago, Jr., "Beyond Tokenism: Women as True Corporate Peers: Can Organization Cope with Male Executives Who Resist Working with Women as Peers?" *Business Horizons*, December 1973, pp. 69–76.

14 Matina Horner, "Toward an Understanding of Achievement Related Conflicts in Women," *Journal of Social Issues*, 1972, pp. 157–176.

15 Cynthia Fuchs Epstein, *Women's Place: Options and Limits in Professional Careers*, Berkeley: University of California Press, 1970.

16 Cynthia Fuchs Epstein, "Encountering the Male Establishment: Sex-Status Limits on Women's Careers in the Professions," *American Journal of Sociology*, May 1970, pp. 965–982.

Chapter II

Sex Differences and Their Implications for Management

Carol Nagy Jacklin
Eleanor Emmons Maccoby

Do sex differences make a difference in management? Does the nature of women make it more likely or less likely that individual women will succeed in management jobs? Are there differences between the sexes that allow us to predict differences in business skills between men and women? Do hormones interfere with a woman's job performance?

We want to summarize some of our findings about psychological sex differences and explore how they relate to women at work, particularly women in management. Let us begin by describing the scope of our work and explaining how it differs from other work on sex differences.*

Most reports on the psychology of men and women emphasize studies in which *differences* between the two sexes have

---

*The complete review and discussion of findings may be found in Maccoby and Jacklin, *The Psychology of Sex Differences*, Stanford, Calif.: Stanford, 1974.

been found. We were interested not only in such studies, but in studies where differences might have been found but were not. Such results are harder to find; they tend to be hidden away in footnotes, omitted from summaries of research, and buried in tables without comment in the text. Clearly, a review that included primarily the positive findings would present a partial (and biased) picture. Therefore we systematically looked through reports of research using subjects of both sexes, and included in our review the studies that found no differences.

Are there consistent sex differences in psychological functioning when both positive and negative findings are tabulated? There are some, but far fewer than assumed. Certain allegations may safely be labeled "myths" since there is clear evidence against them. Other claims have a solid basis in fact. And still others cannot be evaluated without more evidence. We want to discuss the myths and realities and how they might affect both sexes.

A. ACHIEVEMENT MOTIVATION, INTELLIGENCE, AND LEARNING

1. Achievement Motivation

It is commonly believed that if there are not as many women as men among the very high achievers in the professions, this must reflect a lower level of achievement motivation among women—perhaps a lack of interest in achievement that begins during childhood. We have found no evidence to support the view that girls lack achievement motivation. Indeed, the reverse seems true during the school years. Girls on the average seem to maintain a consistent and fairly strong level of academic motivation, while boys tend to defect. Boys' achievement motivation is more responsive than girls' to competitive challenge, and the presence of a competitor is sometimes needed to bring a boy's interest in achieving up to the level where the girl's was initially, but there is every reason to believe that girls care as much as boys do about mastering the intellectual content of their schoolwork.

The sexes are similar in task persistence when this has been measured. It is sometimes alleged that girls achieve for the praise and approval of others, while boys achieve for the sake of sheer intrinsic interest in the task. However, so far this allegation too has turned out to be myth. Both sexes are influenced almost equally by the reactions of parents, teachers, and others to their performance.

Can the different levels of adult achievement of the two sexes be traced to other aspects of their motivation—for example, to self-confidence or self-esteem? Our review has indicated that on a variety of measures of self-esteem, boys and girls present essentially equivalent pictures through childhood and adolescence. During the college years, the situation changes somewhat, however. When college women are asked how well they think they will do on a new task they are about to undertake, or how good their grades will be at the next grading period, they are less optimistic than college men, and this is true on tasks where they do in fact perform as well as men. Furthermore, they have a lesser sense of being in control of their own destinies. The so-called locus-of-control measures reveal higher internal control scores for men than women at college age. The male college student's self-concept is characterized by a sense of personal potency and optimism concerning a variety of task performances, and this may well be relevant to subsequent achievement.

It is important to note that the sex difference in self-concept *does not extend* beyond the college years. We have no information on college-age adults who do not go to college. Studies of graduate students do not show sex differences in self-esteem or self-confidence. Similarly differences in post-college-age adults do not show sex differences.

2. Intelligence

Tests of general intelligence do not show sex differences. This is true partly because several such tests were originally designed to minimize sex differences by choosing a balanced set of items, some of which gave males an advantage, some females, but most being items on which the sexes were known to perform similarly. In subtests of special abilities, however, sex differences do emerge. In general, girls excel at verbal tasks and boys at mathematical and visual-spatial ones. Studies of verbal abilities in

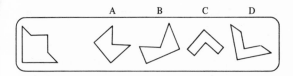

Figure 1.

the 1930s and 1940s indicated that girls' verbal advantage begins very early. More recent work casts doubt upon this conclusion.

There are not many new large-sample studies with children under the age of 2 1/2, and so we do not know whether today's boys and girls differ with respect to the age at which they say their first word or the age at which they first combine words into short sentences. But what recent work is available for children under three does not report a sex difference. Likewise, among children of preschool age, girls are not more verbal except perhaps among disadvantaged children. Among economically average or advantaged children, consistent sex differences in verbal ability only begin to emerge at about ten, with girls forging ahead not only in verbal fluency but in measures of complex, high-level verbal skills as well. Estimates vary greatly on the degree of sex difference found during the teen-age years, but a reasonable conclusion is that the girls score about one-fourth of a standard deviation higher than boys on most measures.

On measures of mathematical ability, few sex differences appear before early adolescence, except again among disadvantaged children, where girls do better on tests of number concepts and arithmetical skills. In adolescence, among unselected populations of children, boys generally score higher on such tests than girls, but how much higher is very difficult to say from present evidence. Thus we reiterate a firm and venerable finding, that boys do excel in math, while noting that the difference does not emerge until relatively late in development and that its magnitude has not been established.

In a similar vein, the sex difference in visual-spatial ability continues to be a widely replicable fact. Visual-spatial skills are involved, for example, in tasks where the subject must mentally rotate one figure to see whether it fits into another figure. Figure 1 shows an item from the Primary Mental Abilities subtest on spatial ability. The subject's task is to identify which of the figures in the set on the right would make a complete square if fitted into the figure on the left. Embedded-figures tests also call for spatial ability. In these tests, the subject is shown a simple figure and must find its outlines when it is embedded in a larger, more complex figure (see Figure 2).

After approximately the age of ten or twelve, boys do better than girls on such tests on the average, although, of course, some girls obtain very high scores and some boys do poorly. Embedded figures tests suitable for younger children have been developed, and while some children solve them much more easily than others, the variations in ability are usually not related to sex.

It is worth noting that the greater skill adolescent boys display on the embedded figures test should not be taken to mean a generalized superiority in analytic thought process. Girls do as well (or better) on tasks that call for other forms of disembedding, or "decontextualization," and their limitation seems solely in the visual-spatial sphere.

One of the most intriguing unsolved problems in the whole area of sex differences is the relationship of hormones to intellectual performance. So far there is no information on the relation of female hormones to intellectual performance, but increasing evidence shows a negative correlation among male subjects between male hormones and spatial performance, and perhaps to other kinds of intellectual performance as well. Why, then, is it precisely during the early years of adolescence, when there is a massive increase in male hormones, that there is also an upward spurt in performance on spatial tasks? There have

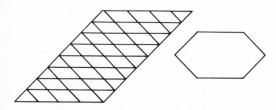

Figure 2.

been some ingenious efforts to make sense of this situation, but they have not as yet produced a convincing solution.

3. Learning

It has been argued (Broverman et al., 1968) that females are superior to males in tasks that call for "simple, overlearned, repetitive behavior," while males excel in "complex behaviors requiring problem solving, delay, or reversal of usual habits." This hypothesis must be very closely scrutinized, for if it were true, it would have vast implications for the kinds of job training or any other training of men and women.

Simple conditioning is a learning process at which females should excel, if the differential is valid. We have examined the work in infant conditioning, conditioning of avoidance or other responses in preschoolers, and conditioning of verbal responses in children and adults. The results are clear: the two sexes are remarkably alike in their response to conditioning procedures, and sex differences are almost never found in the speed of acquisition of a conditioned response, nor in the rate of extinction. The single exception is in eyelid conditioning among adults, where women condition more readily (by blinking to signaled puffs of air to the eye). As Spence and Spence (1966) have shown, however, eyelid conditioning is faster among subjects who score high on the Manifest Anxiety Scale, and women on the average score higher than men on this scale. When eyelid conditioning is done under "masked" conditions—that is, when it is incidental to procedures which are presumably intended to measure something else—the sex differences disappear, and so do the correlations with the Manifest Anxiety Scale. Thus it would appear that we are dealing with a sex difference in manifest anxiety, not with a difference in ease of conditioning.

What other kind of learning might fall into the category of simple rote learning? Paired-comparisons learning might be a good candidate, although we know that subjects frequently complicate this process by imposing their own elaborate hypotheses upon it. In any case, we find that there is no consistent sex difference in speed or accuracy of paired-associates learning.

What about learning tasks that call for problem solving,

delay, or the reversal of usual habits? Do such tasks give an advantage to males? It is difficult to get agreement on which tasks call for inhibition of previously acquired response tendencies. To our minds, even such a simple process as discriminating learning calls for such inhibition, and this is a task as to which sex differences are almost never found. A clearer case would be reversal shifts, where a choice previously labeled as "correct" is made systematically incorrect. No sex differences have been found in studies of reversal shifts. Similarly studies involving delay of reinforcement call for response inhibition. We were able to locate only four delay-of-reinforcement studies that analyzed for sex of subject—none found a sex difference. The Stroop Color-Word Test (1935) might be considered an excellent instrument for testing response inhibition—when a subject looks at the word green printed in red ink, for example, and is asked to "read" the name of the ink color, he must inhibit a strongly learned tendency to read the printed word. There seems to be little recent work using this test, but the initial work with it reported that subjects of the two sexes did not differ in their skill on the task.

It is not necessary to belabor the point: we have found absolutely no evidence to support the theory that women perform intellectual tasks in a rote, repetitive way, while men are using more complex problem-solving strategies that involve inhibiting old responses in the interests of acquiring new ones. Both sexes do shift toward higher-level problem-solving strategies from childhood to adulthood, but they do so at the same rate and with equal success.

B. SOCIABILITY AND AGGRESSION

1. Sociability and Affiliation

What about social skills? It has been alleged that women are more dependent than men, that women are more likely to ask for help or to cling to others in the face of a challenge or threat, while men engage in active problem solving with or without the mediation of others. Women are said to find security in the company of others and therefore to be more "social" than men, more oriented toward social stimulation, more responsive to social reinforcement or the danger of losing social approval, and more likely to seek proximity to others than to work independently. If these allegations are true, then we might expect women's performance to differ when asked to work alone or in a group. We wish to evaluate any sex differences in sociability that might affect interpersonal relations and women's job performance.

Are girls and women especially concerned about being liked, or loved, by others? Are women more sensitive to the opinions of others, and more sociable—more likely to seek the company of others, less comfortable when alone? We have been surprised at how little basis in fact there is for these beliefs. In infancy neither sex has been shown to have more interest than the other in social (as compared with nonsocial) stimuli; nor, as already noted, is one sex more susceptible than the other to praise or criticism for performance on intellectual tasks. Beyond this, our review has shown that there is no consistent tendency for little girls to be more attached to their parents or "dependent" on them.

Children of both sexes seek to be close to parents, particularly under stressful conditions, but they are equally ready to leave their parents to explore a novel environment. There is some evidence that in early childhood boys are more likely to cry when left alone by a parent, but this sex difference would be transitory. When it comes to play with age mates, girls are *not* more social than boys, if by this we mean the amount of time spent interacting with others as contrasted with solitary play. In fact, the balance is tipped toward a higher level of social interaction among boys, at least during the preschool years. The sexes do differ in the nature of their social interests during childhood, but the difference seems to be qualitative rather than quantitative: boys congregate in larger groups, while girls tend to prefer twosomes and threesomes as friendship groupings, especially after they enter school.

Women are widely believed to be more empathic—that is, more tuned in to the emotional states of others—and more likely to go to the aid of others who are in need of help. But the evidence simply does not permit such a conclusion. Empathy is not an easy quality to measure; most research focuses on whether a subject can accurately identify the emotion that someone else is feeling, without regard to whether the onlooker *shares* the emotional state of the other. In the rather sparse research that has been done so far, the two sexes have proved to be equally adept at identifying the emotional states of others. Furthermore, there is no real tendency for either sex to be more altruistic in the sense of alleviating another's distress or making efforts to provide gratification to others. Whether a person goes to another's aid in Good Samaritan rescues depends upon what kind of aid is needed, and also upon whether the person to be aided is of the same or opposite sex as the helper.

In summary, there are very few differences between the sexes in social relation skills. The male potential for empathic and svmpathetic emotional reactions and the male potential for kindly, helpful behavior toward others (including children) seem to have been seriously underrated.

2. Aggression and Dominance

So far we have dealt largely with widely held beliefs about psychological sex differences that are not supported by examination of all available evidence. We turn now to an area where sex differences are clear and quite consistent with what is widely believed: namely, aggression. Males *are* more aggressive than females, and this is true from approximately the age of two years. The sex difference is found in a very wide range of measurement situations, in observation of free play in naturalistic settings as well as in the laboratory; furthermore, the results do not seem to depend on the measure of aggression employed. It is widely believed that boys show more physical aggression and girls more verbal aggression, but this proves not to be the case. Boys have a higher level of verbal as well as physical aggression. An exchange of verbal insults frequently precedes an exchange of blows, and boys frequently use verbal taunts or threats in the process of working out dominance relations in boys' play groups. It is also widely believed that the two sexes may be equivalent in their underlying potential for aggressive behavior but that girls inhibit the outward displays of aggression because they are more likely to have been punished for it.

This point of view is supported in work by Bandura (1965) and his colleagues, in which it was shown that girls were less likely to imitate an aggressive model spontaneously, but if offered a reward for imitating all the model's responses they could remember, they proved to have learned a great deal more about the model's aggression than could have been guessed from their spontaneous imitations. It is alleged that this finding implies that if the sanctions imposed on girls' aggression were removed, girls would be as aggressive as boys.

We have several objections to this point of view: there is now no reason to believe that girls are more often punished for aggression. Indeed, the reverse may well be the case. Observational work in nursery schools indicates that boys draw more negative reactions to their aggression than girls, both in absolute numbers of reprimands and punishments and proportionally to the number of aggressive acts they commit. Furthermore, if girls' normally low level of aggression were a result of inhibitions laid over a fairly high aggressive potential, we would expect to find girls being aggressive in ways and situations where there would not be repercussions for it. Yet males manifest considerably more than females all the forms of attenuated and displaced aggression—fantasy aggression, playful aggression (where a punch on the shoulder is accompanied by a grin)—and probably in bullying toward younger children and animals. A finding by Titley and Viney (1969) is relevant here: they used the Buss shock technique, where the subject acts as an experimenter's assistant and is asked to administer shocks to a learner when the learner makes a mistake. The duration and intensity of shocks a subject administers are his aggression score. Male subjects characteristically administer longer and stronger shocks to their victims than do female subjects. Titley and Viney used a physically handicapped learner in one condition of this experiment. They found that the victim's obvious helplessness increased the intensity of shocks delivered by males but decreased the shocks given by females. This and other research undermines the picture of a high level of bottled-up aggression in females that is only waiting for a safe outlet. We believe that the readiness of women and girls to respond aggressively, either overtly or covertly, is simply not as great as it is among males.

There are several indications of biological underpinning for the sex difference in aggression: this differential is found in all human societies in which aggression has been studied, greater aggression is found consistently among the animals closest to man in the phylogenetic series, and levels of aggression are linked to the amount of male hormones present in the individuals being studied. The use of mainly correlational evidence here must be avoided. One can take blood samples from a group of males and analyze them for current levels of androgens. Rose et al. (1971, 1972) have found that with both monkeys and human beings such scores yield positive correlations with some (but not other) behavioral measures of aggression. However, a high androgen level can be both a result and a cause of aggressive behavior. That is, if a normally meek animal is placed with a cage mate whom he can dominate in aggressive encounters, his testosterone level goes up and remains up until he is placed with a cage mate who defeats him. The causal contribution of male hormones to aggression is more clearly demonstrated by studies in which male hormones have been experimentally administered; in such studies, the elevated aggression levels of individuals of both sexes do testify to the power of male hormones in increasing the incidence of aggressive behavior.

An interesting facet of aggression studies has to do with the choice of victims. Not only do females initiate aggressive encounters less frequently than males, but also, among both animals and human beings, females are less frequent victims. That is, male aggression is aimed primarily at other males. Patterson and his colleagues (1967) have done some detailed analyses of aggressive sequences between pairs of children in nursery school; they have found that, in general, aggression toward a particular victim will be increased if that victim cries, yields a disputed toy, or otherwise thus reinforces the aggressive actions of the attacker. Girls, when aggressed against, responded as frequently as did boys with reinforcing behavior; yet aggressive acts toward girls tended not to be continued or repeated. Thus it was not girls' behavior as targets of aggression that discouraged their aggressors.

In many people's minds, aggression and dominance are closely linked. We know among apes that dominance is achieved and maintained through either aggression of threats thereof. If among humans the male is more aggressive, does this mean that he must dominate the human female? The answer turns out to be complex but mainly negative. Although boys make more attempts at dominance than girls do, most of these attempts are directed toward one another, or (less often) toward adults. Boys rather seldom attempt to dominate girls; when they do, the evidence is contradictory as to whether they are likely to succeed. The bulk of the evidence shows that girls do not yield readily to boys' dominance attempts. Among children from age four or five up to adolescence, play groups tend to be sex-segregated; dominance issues occur more frequently in boys' play groups, and among young boys, at least, dominance appears to depend on "toughness," including fighting ability.

As children grow older, it is more and more difficult to find a single dominance hierarchy. An individual who has a leadership position in one activity is not especially likely to have it in another. Furthermore, fighting ability declines in importance (in most kinds of groups) in determining who will have leadership. In adulthood, there appears to be little or no relationship between dominance and aggression. To summarize this point: dominance, or leadership, appears to be achieved primarily by aggressive means among apes and little boys. Among human beings, the linkage weakens with increasing maturity, and there appears to be no intrinsic reason why the more aggressive sex should be the dominant one in adult relationships.

C. HORMONES, CYCLES, MOODS, AND BEHAVIOR

Are women slaves to their hormonal systems? Does the familiar premenstrual syndrome involve some incapacity to make rational decisions or otherwise function fully? There certainly is evidence that hormones and moods are related. What is not widely known is that this is not a sex difference. Male hormones are cyclical too, and moods are known to fluctuate with these hormones.

In recent work at the Stanford Medical School (Doering et al., 1974), hormones and moods were assessed every other day for sixty days on a group of twenty men from nineteen to fifty years of age. Half the subjects studied showed clear evidence of cycles of both hormones and moods. The cycles varied in length from fourteen to thirty days, and as is the case in women, some men showed dramatic mood-hormone relations while others did not. The researchers concluded that a four-month study would probably have revealed recurring cycles for all their subjects. The cycles they could document led them to speculate that the average male cycle length would probably approximate twenty-eight days.

Our hormonal systems are complex. Much more research is needed before we will be able to understand the complete picture. For example, the percentage change of testosterone in males is smaller than the percentage change of estrogens in women, but estrogen changes have not yet been measured in males. We know that some hormones are more biologically active than others, but we simply don't know how different hormones work together or counter each other in our systems.

Male and female hormone cycles may differ only in that (1) there is a greater variability in male cycle length and (2) there are external signs of the female cycle. Both of these differences for girls and women may actually be an advantage. A woman can more easily take her cycle into account in understanding her own mood swings. One could then argue that the male hormone mood cycle is more dangerous, since a man cannot as readily take it into account and deal accordingly with his hostile feelings.

Hormones and moods are controllable. Women and men do cope with their hormones and moods in their work and personal lives. Women do not in fact weep at the office one or two days each month, and men do not punch their fellows. It may be that the more responsibility men and women have in a situation, the more they feel compelled to cope with their hormone-mood swing. Male and female, in other words, all human (and probably all animal), behavior is related to hormones. But it is a mistake to believe that this is somehow a "women's problem."

D. SEX DIFFERENCES AND MANAGEMENT

We have sorted out a number of myths and some fairly well-documented realities about the psychological characteristics of the two sexes. We have noted many respects in which males and females are more alike than is commonly supposed. Of the differences between the two, some seem more than others to be attributable to social shaping. Even when biologically based differences are found, the variations within each sex are so large that many individuals reflect characteristics more commonly associated with the opposite sex. Furthermore, even behavior to which an individual is biologically predisposed will not develop unless and until appropriate learning takes place. Behavior is always subject to shaping by societal forces. Any disposition is likely to manifest itself under a rather narrow set of eliciting conditions, and not take the form of a generalized "trait."

Does the existence of some dispositions that have biological foundations commit us to the view that the two sexes are destined to have different status roles and occupations in life? Or that there is reason to expect one sex or the other to have some advantage in management? It would be very difficult to make the case that most traditionally male occupations call especially for spatial or mathematical ability, or that "women's work" calls for verbal ability. With rare exceptions, the work assignments to the two sexes are made along wholly different lines. In the case of a professional prizefighter it is clear that the male's greater strength and aggressiveness are required. Here, inevitably, men will continue to be predominant. However, in some societies, e.g., where only the women bear heavy burdens upon their heads or do the heavy agricultural labor, the division of labor between the sexes often means that women perform greater feats of physical strength during their daily lives than men. Perhaps women, with their lower levels of strength and aggression, have been less willing or less able to protest onorous assignments.

In our judgment only one sex difference might be related to management skills: aggression. Our question becomes, Are aggression and concern for dominance necessary or useful in management today?

What about aggressive leadership? When we speak of an aggressive leader, we are not speaking of an individual's tendency to verbally or physically attack subordinates, peers, or superiors. We are rather speaking of the person's willingness to tackle challenging assignments. As we have indicated earlier, there is no evidence of sex differences in achievement motivation, in risk taking, in task persistence, or in other related skills. Therefore there is no reason to believe there are sex differences in aggressive leadership.

What about competitiveness and dominance attempts? Boys do make more attempts to dominate peers and adults and are more responsive in some (but by no means all) competitive situations. There are trends in management which suggest that competitiveness and dominance may not necessarily be the most productive management style (Johnson and Ouchi, 1974). Management teams and decision-making and problem-solving groups are becoming a familiar part of organizations. The success of such teams demands the cooperation of managers to deal with problems too complex for any one person to handle. In such situations, competitiveness could pose a threat to the team's functioning. Women may be particularly effective in organizations using team management. But we are speculating. At this time there is no information on this issue, and it is an area where research could and should be done. In summary, nothing in the above discussion suggests that acquisition of all available leadership positions by men is inevitable or desirable. Leadership skills are varied; women are as capable as men of developing relevant competencies in organizations where leadership is achieved through skill in setting achievable goals, in planning, organizing, persuading, conciliating, and conveying enthusiasm. We see no reason for a sex bias.

One last psychological fact about women *and* men. Change is difficult, but seldom as difficult as it seems before it is made. Men who have worked with women are more likely to favor placing women in management positions. The less actual experience men have had working with women, the harder they think such a transition would be (Bowman et al., 1965). This is a specific example of a general psychological phenomenon. The best way to change stereotypes about any group is to give people experience with that group (Bem, 1970).

Leadership, task persistence, achievement motivation, intellectual abilities, and many other psychological abilities do not favor one sex over the other for job performance. Women are not psychologically handicapped for positions in management. Recruiting, hiring, and promotion policies have handicapped women. Not for much longer, we hope.

REFERENCES

Bandura, A., "Influence of Models' Reinforcement Contingencies on the Acquisition of Imitative Responses," *Journal of Personality and Social Psychology*, vol. 1, 1965, pp. 589–595.

Bem, D.: *Beliefs, Attitudes, and Human Affairs*, Belmont, Calif.: Brooks/Cole, 1970.

Bowman, G. W., N. B. Worthy, and S. A. Greyser, "Are Women Executive People?" *Harvard Business Review*, July–August 1965, pp. 14–28, 164–178.

Broverman, D. M., E. L. Klaiber, Y. Kobayashi, and W. Vogel, "Roles of Activation and Inhibition in Sex Differences in Cognitive Abilities," *Psychological Review*, vol. 75, 1968, pp. 23–50.

Doering, C. H., H. R. H. Brodie, T. Kraemer, H. Becker, and D. A. Hamburg, "Plasma Testosterone Levels and Psychologic Measures in Men over a Two-Month Period," in R. C. Friedman and R. M. Richart (eds.), *Sex Differences in Behavior*, New York: Wiley, 1974.

Johnson, R. T., and W. G. Ouchi, "Made in America (under Japanese Management)," *Harvard Business Review*, September–October 1974, pp. 61–69.

Patterson, G. R., R. A. Littman, and W. Bricker, "Assertive Behavior in Children: A Step toward a Theory of Aggression," *Monographs of the Society for Research in Child Development*, vol. 32, 1967.

Rose, R. M., T. P. Gordon, and I. S. Bernstein, "Plasma Testosterone Levels in the Male Rhesus: Influences of Sexual and Social Stimuli," *Science*, vol. 178, 1972, pp. 643–645.

Rose, R. M., J. W. Holaday, and I. S. Bernstein, "Plasma, Testosterone, Dominance Rank, and Aggressive Behavior in Male Rhesus Monkeys," *Nature*, vol. 231, 1971, pp. 366–368.

Spence, K. W., and J. T. Spence, "Sex and Anxiety Differences in Eyelid Conditioning," *Psychological Bulletin*, vol. 65, 1966, pp. 137–142.

Stroop, J. R., "Studies of Interference in Serial Verbal Reactions," *Journal of Experimental Psychology*, vol. 6, 1935, pp. 643–662.

Titley, R. W., and W. Viney, "Expression of Aggression toward the Physically Handicapped," *Perceptual and Motor Skills*, vol. 29, 1969, pp. 51–56.

Chapter III

The Executive
Man and Woman:
The Issue of Sexuality

David L. Bradford
Alice G. Sargent
Melinda S. Sprague

When the issue of hiring women in management arises, a frequent response from male executives is joking about the sexual implications: "Won't that make field trips more interesting!" "No woman would be safe in this office with Bill here." Such comments enrage advocates of affirmative action, who see the issue as one of fairness and the opportunity for options other than housewife or secretary. We believe the problem of women in management is complex, encompassing far more than sexual interplay, but this joking reveals more than simple prejudice. Many of the difficulties men and women experience in their relationships at work revolve around sexuality.

Sexuality covers a wide area, and so initially we need to distinguish several ways sex influences managerial behavior. The first refers to the effect of *differential socialization* of males and females. This socialization covers a wide area of which only a part relates to sexual behavior per se. A substantial body of research demonstrates that from birth boys and girls are consistently treated differently. The types of games, toys, and books given to boys, as well as the kind of behavior for which boys are rewarded and punished, teach boys different values, aspirations, and behavioral skills than girls. Boys are supported for being aggressive, assertive, analytical, and competitive, while girls are praised for being helpful, passive, deferential, and concerned with interpersonal relationships.

Teachers as well as parents support these differences. One example is the research by Serbin (1973), who found that elementary school teachers, both male and female, responded more often to questions raised by boys than girls, and gave the boys longer answers that were richer in content. Girls received more perfunctory answers often accompanied by a pat on the head or arm around the shoulder—as if support and not cognitive content were the important response. Little wonder that this differential training is excellent preparation for men to succeed in management while handicapping women who want to travel the same route.

By college the differences are learned well. Aries (in press) found in a mixed sex group of college students that men typically talked two-thirds of the time. When women did communicate, they directed their comments to men rather than to other women and were more concerned about acceptance and relationships while men were more attuned to authority and impressing each other.

A second way sex influences managerial behavior is through *stereotypes* of the other sex. Definite expectations exist regarding the values, interests, aptitudes, and abilities of a person just because the other happens to be male or female. Women, as well as men, often expect other women to be interested in fashion design, not finance, and in personnel, not line management. Managers assume that a married woman will not want out-of-town job assignments while such consideration is not given to a married man.

Many times, expectations about competence levels differ solely on the basis of sex, so that the *same* output is often judged of lower quality when observers believe it to have been done by a woman rather than a man. Goldberg (1968) and Pheterson et al. (1971) found that females also have lower expectations of a woman's competence. In these studies women evaluated paintings and written reports as of lesser quality when they bore a female signature than when a male's. Clearly, these perceptions and expectations influence the type of job assignments male supervisors allocate, the performance level they expect, the way they assess tasks performed, and the candidates they consider when opportunities for advancement arise. Fear of failure may be a major concern for most men, but Horner's (1970) research on college students found that because women are punished for success by being ostracized by other women and rejected by men, they are ambivalent about success. In fact, in Horner's research college women and black men demonstrated a comparable conflict.

The third area deals with how *sexuality* per se influences how men and women work together. Sexuality here refers not just to sexual attraction and office affairs but to the various ways in which a male manager sees himself as a sexual male and responds to the sexuality of a female coworker—and the ways a female manager experiences her own sexuality in responding to males.

This article will focus on this third area of sexuality and discuss the following four aspects: (1) the way that men define and measure their masculinity and females their femininity, and the relation of these self-images to work success; (2) the sexual messages behind many male-female interactions; (3) the likelihood that introducing females to all levels of management will be disruptive to the way men commonly relate to other men; and (4) the matter of mutual attraction leading to sexual intercourse. Obviously these four aspects do not apply to all males or females in management, nor is each necessarily of the same intensity as one moves from first-level supervision to the executive suite. What we are suggesting is that sexuality in one form or other helps to explain why managers feel ambivalent about affirmative action for women, why many men and women have difficulty relating to each other in the office, and why women executives are handicapped in their search for success.

A. HOW SEXUALITY IS DEFINED

1. Masculinity and Work Success: The Compatible Equation

An important aspect of the sense of self-identity for both males and females is their masculinity and femininity. The charge of not being masculine is as devastating an attack for a man as questioning a woman's femininity is for a woman. How do males assert their sexuality? Teen-agers resort to fistfighting, playing "chicken" with cars, playing football, and competing against one another to see who can consume more beer or have more dates. While this may do for youth, an educated adult must find more discreet and indirect proofs.

For many men, work serves as the major vehicle defining their identity, including sexual identity. A job indicates not only a person's competence and worth but even who he is. When people meet socially, one of the first questions asked is, "What do you do?", for the answer is seen as telling a great deal about the individual. Being a plumber or a physicist, an executive or an engineer, is perceived as saying a lot about the individual's values, abilities, personality, and worth. Conversely, as Bakke's (1934) work of the Depression showed, being unemployed has a detrimental effect on a person's self-image and worth.

Status and pay of the job also bear an element of sexuality. The lumberjack and construction worker exemplify the rough masculinity of physical labor, but there is an aura of sexuality around success itself, as most clearly seen with famous individuals whose power and male sexuality are highly correlated. Not only does sexuality frequently contain elements of competition, dominance, and power, but power often takes on sexual implications. Even some of the terms used for the former are borrowed from the latter. A person's program is said to have been "emasculated" by a certain decision, and the manager who fails is described as "impotent."

This equation of power with affirmation of masculine sexuality relates not only to the type of occupation, but also to specific task accomplishments on the job. Not infrequently a task dispute in a staff meeting takes on an overtone of interpersonal rivalry, often with a *macho* flavor. Logical arguments, the pros and cons of various positions, can mean more than just arriving at the best solution. Certainly there are other motives at work so that the "winner" feels more competent and valued by the organization, but we suggest he might also feel more masculine and reaffirmed as a man. Men once dueled physically, but now verbal wit and repartee have replaced the sword. In academic circles this has been perfected to an art, where logical arguments between colleagues are the forum for dominance.*

For men and for the women who admire them and help them stage these roles, there is congruence between sexuality and work performance. This refers not only to the compatibility between how boys are socialized (i.e., raised to be verbally aggressive, competitive, concerned with the task more than the relationship) and requirements of the workplace, but also to a similar congruence between work success and affirmation of masculinity. Thus men strive to advance, build up their programs, and compete in meetings partially to obtain status and financial records that connote masculine success, but also to affirm their masculinity more directly. Even those who do not use success for sexual reassurance may feel threatened as males if they experience work failure.

This perception of the overlap between sexuality and professional success may help to explain some of the opposition to the advancement of women. To lose to a woman is inevitably more shattering to a male's self-image than to be bested by another male. Men often apply the term "castrating" to an aggressive or competent female, implying that her intentions are to lessen the masculinity of the male. But the same action or behavior may vary in its apparent impact depending on whether it comes from a male or female colleague. Behavior that is acceptable in a man is denigrated in a woman. A man may be assertive, but a woman is overly aggressive. A man may attack, but a woman castrates! Are there that many women who really try to destroy the

*Another sign that verbal arguments can have a sexually competitive component is the behavior that not infrequently arises when an attractive female is in an otherwise all-male group. While she is not directly addressed, the men compete among themselves to see who is wittiest and sharpest.

masculinity of male coworkers? Or is the real issue that because so many men make the connection, often unconsciously, between their masculinity and job performance, any assertiveness or task success by women is experienced by the male as a threat at that level?

2. The Perceived Incompatibility of Femininity and Work Success

This problem or dilemma exists for women not [handwritten annotation]

Task competence and sexuality interact for women as well, but for women an incompatibility exists between behaviors intrinsic to task success. Such traits include being passive, acting emotionally, being supportive, and relating well to others. Since high school, many women have felt a conflict between "being competent" and "being popular." These women must find validation of their sexuality elsewhere, since the charge of nonfemininity is a common response to any show of competence by a woman.

The options are not very satisfying for women who feel this dilemma. One alternative is to hold back from expressing competence or to express it through others. The latter ploy may mean saying things through a male, preferably the boss, so that he and others think it is his idea. When a woman does present an idea or suggestion, it is often in a deferential manner without the assurance or bluster that enables men to get their ideas accepted. Furthermore, when her idea is attacked, she is more likely to concede than to rebut: even when a woman can have ideas, she is not expected to defend them very staunchly. These evasions help some women to preserve their femininity, as traditionally defined, but at the cost of inhibiting competence.

The other extreme is forfeiting acceptance as a female to facilitate the more direct expression of ability. This is the stereotype of the "iron maiden" who is so determined to battle it out in the man's world that any warmth or softness is suppressed.*

These are extreme positions, whereas in actuality most

---

*Henning (1974) reports that a not infrequent occurrence for the woman who has gone this route is, around age forty, to realize the personal cost and begin to express the warmth and softness so long suppressed.

females in the managerial world work out a solution somewhere in between. Clearly this dilemma exists for women but not for men. The male executive, finding work and sexuality synergistic, does not have to spend time and energy working out a compromise. Furthermore, the very term "compromise" implies some concession whereby competence and/or sexual self-identity is lessened in the resolution.

B. MALE-FEMALE RELATIONSHIPS

The way males and females relate to one another at work has a sexual component in that the behavior of each is constantly influenced by the sex of the other. Most obviously this occurs when that person is viewed in terms of sexual attractiveness. One manager put it this way: "I don't know whether it's right for me to act this way, or whether it makes me a Male Chauvinist Pig, but the first time I meet a woman, I respond to her as a sexual object and only later as a person." We are not suggesting that all males or females have this same initial orientation, but even with those who don't, their interactions with the opposite sex have a sexual component even when sexual attraction is not involved.

In our culture certain ritualized ways of relating to the opposite sex have developed that have their roots in courtship behavior. For men, this may take the form of respectful deference to the "fair sex." Or it could include a protectiveness and solicitousness. To illustrate this point, imagine the following incident at a cocktail party. Three men have been discussing the state of the economy when a woman joins their group. They pull in their stomachs, stand a little straighter, and shift the subject to some mild flirtatious bantering, compliments on her attire, or some solicitous query about the family. If the conversation moves back to business, it would not be unusual to see some competitive jostling among the men to determine who sounds more astute, and attempts to one-up the other. Approving comments from the female are welcomed, inane comments tolerated, but highly perceptive comments from her would certainly produce astonishment. It would be even more unsettling if she were to disagree with one of the males on a business issue, particularly if she were to correct him. If the male thus corrected replied defensively, the others would rush to her defense.

Yet this is a cocktail party. So what if the men are showing off a bit to the female present? What harm is there in some mild flirting? What is wrong with chivalry? And what does this scenario say about sexuality and women in management?

This interaction reinforces, in the minds of all of those involved, the woman's inferior position. She is expected to be naive and submissive, ignorant about business matters, unable to take care of herself and therefore in need of a man for protection. But if she is to be successful in the work world, she must learn how to operate in that more hostile environment. Passivity and deference will not get her far. One woman described it thusly: "None of the behaviors I learned from watching my mother talk to my father are helpful at work. In fact, they are dysfunctional."

The type of relating described at the cocktail party reflects the typical courtship behavior that is part of the dating-relating game males and females have engaged in since puberty. The problem is that such interaction has permeated society. Being influenced and responding either consciously or unconsciously to the sexuality of the other is the primary way men and women have learned to relate to each other.*

1. Roles and Their Uses

The problem is that this set of attitudes and behavior cannot be confined to the date or cocktail party but carries over to the office. It is most clearly seen between the manager and *his* secretary. The mild flirtation, compliments on her new hair style,

*If this seems a bit farfetched to the reader, we would like to suggest the following exercise. The next time you observe a male and female interacting, change the sex of the woman so that "he" is using the same words, tone, gesture, and way of relating. It works just as well to change the man's sex instead. In either case, having the two be of the same sex produces a jarring effect. In both cases the sexuality will become apparent, for with the sex the "same," the interaction takes on a homosexual flavor.

perfume, or dress, is part and parcel of the daily interaction.* As long as it is verbal, this interaction probably causes few problems and is the kind of friendly banter that makes interaction between the sexes enjoyable. But this mode of relating may not be limited to occasional kidding. It may underly much of the relationship between males and females on the management level.

This kind of relationship is not attributable solely to the male; the tendency exists in both directions. The female is aware that she is relating to males and acts accordingly. Thus men and women get locked into reciprocal roles that have a semisexual basis. While not the only ways that they interact, the following four role relationships are illustrative of the assertion that ways of relating developed on the outside carry over to the office in a manner that limits the potential of both parties by isolating the person and limiting the range of behavior rather than encouraging the full scope of self-expression.†

a. The *Macho* and the Seductress The primary mode of relating for these two roles is sexual. Actual seduction may not occur, but the nature of their interaction usually has a sexual flavor with elements of flirting and game playing. The man is concerned that women see and value him as a potent male and makes constant verbal efforts to emphasize this. He frequently attempts to assert his dominance over the woman by kidding with her about her attractiveness and then by putting her down for her incompetence in some other area. The cost to the woman is that she is seen more as a sexual object than as a person who has

*Note that a similar relationship between a female manager and her *male* secretary would not be deemed quite appropriate, because that contradicts rather than complements the organizational hierarchy for a male is usually dominant sexually. The quasi-sexual aspect of the boss-secretary relationship not infrequently develops between a person with a great deal of power and his personal assistant. A major politician, top executive, or company president may never think of having sexual intercourse with his personal secretary, but part of her devotion and loyalty is based on more than her job responsibilities.

†This analysis owes much to the thinking of Rosabeth Kanter (1974), who developed the concept of stereotypic roles women play in male-dominated settings. "Seductress," "Pet," and "Mother" are her terms.

business-related knowledge and competence. The satisfaction for both is that it reaffirms their sexuality.

The Seductress role is similar for the woman. In some cases she is actively seeking affirmation that she is sexually desirable and wants to have men respond to her as highly attractive. At times men place her in that role and respond to her as potentially available. Being Seductress, either through her own efforts or the expectations of men, gives her great power, for she confers potency on those men to whom she gives approval. This role has the advantage for the woman of affirming her femininity, but it inhibits direct expression of competence.

The presence of such a woman, particularly if there are only one or two females in the group, can be an energizer as the men compete for her approval, but such a situation rapidly becomes dysfunctional if there is a highly interdependent task which requires collaboration. In addition, the competence of the woman is not fully available, since her concern is to be valued as an attractive woman, not as a skilled colleague.

b. Chivalrous Knight and Helpless Maiden This is perhaps the most common set of roles, for they are highly engrained in our culture. Here the male sees himself as stronger and more competent than women and responsible for them. While politely tolerant of women, and respectful of them as women, he would not perceive a woman as having many task-related skills. Consequently he would be less likely to challenge her or make the same demands on her that he would on males.

With this relationship the female, playing the role of Helpless Maiden, can use these stereotypes to manipulate the male for her own ends. Korda (1972) quotes just such a person.

> . . . When it's a question of using my sex, I use it. I don't mean I sleep around—I don't. But if you have any kind of looks and you're not scared yourself you can get what you want. You listen to them, flirt a little, cry when things go wrong, and say, "Gee, I wish you could show me how to do this, you know so much more about this than I do." It's a snap. [p. 29]

Rather than truly being helpless and withdrawing from the

competition, the Helpless Maiden in this case feigns ineptness and derives a sense of power because men serve her. Many men become furious at having become ensnared into this protective stance, for the woman is taking his stereotype, usually used to legitimize female subservience, and turning it against him for her own advantage. To add insult to injury, the very beliefs the men hold—that give Helpless Maiden her power—prevent men from directly confronting her and calling her on this game. To do so would be to treat her like a strong, competent person, i.e., another male. The damage to the Helpless Maiden is great, too. She may "overlearn" these behaviors and never get free of them, losing the opportunity to learn to take care of herself. This reinforces her dependency on a man, which limits her mobility as she fails to develop the direct assertiveness necessary for self-expression and success in the work world.

c. Protective Father and the Pet A combination that crops up, particularly between an older man and younger woman, is a protective father-daughter relationship. This differs from the Knight-Maiden in that the Father tends to be more active in assuming a protective role and the woman's dependence is less likely to be a means of manipulation. The Pet functions almost as a cheerleader for the men she works with. If the Pet, or mascot, goes to lunch with a group of men, she laughs at their jokes, encourages them to talk about themselves and their ideas, but rarely contributes to the content herself.

Not infrequently the Pet and the Seductress get linked with high-status males, which increases the power of both. As in the case of the Seductress, this can validate the Pet's femininity, but at the cost of not being able to show competence directly. The two roles differ in that the Pet, like the overdeveloped but underaged teen-ager, is not perceived as sexually available.

d. Tough Warrior and Nurturant Mother For many men, masculinity is defined in the "John Wayne" tradition of being tough and independent and suppressing all emotions. While functional at times for occupational success, this role definition is costly. This artificial self-sufficiency not only has personal costs, but can interfere with task success as well. Work requires collaboration as well as competition, interdependence as well as independence, and giving and receiving of support and help as well as giving and receiving of ideas.

The reciprocal of this role is that of the Nurturant Mother who serves as the confidante to whom others can bring their problems and seek support. While they are not relating to her as a sexual object, they do not respond to her as a total person; rather they respond to one aspect of the female stereotype. At least, this role removes her from sexual competition, but as Kanter points out, it has three major costs: (1) she is valued because of the support and service she can provide to the males and not because of her individual abilities or actions—thus it tends to cut down on her tendency to take independent initiative around task areas; (2) she often is placed in the role of the "good, accepting mother," which inhibits the extent to which she can use her critical abilities; and (3) she becomes the specialist in emotional issues and shields men from accepting responsibility in their areas; this division of labor serves to further the stereotype that men are rational and logical while women are overly emotional.

We have given these four descriptions of male-female roles as examples of how each can be trapped when relating to the other. While they have been paired, each can exist without the counterpart. A man can play Chivalrous Knight even when none of the women are acting helpless. These roles are overlearned from a multitude of past situations, and so the mere fact of being the only woman present might encourage a woman's tendency to nurture others without any of the men turning to her for support. But it is also likely that a dominant style from one sex evokes the reciprocal in the other. It is difficult to be *Macho* to the Nurturant Mother but easy if the woman is playing Seductress.

Clearly not all interactions are of this type, for people of the opposite sex can relate to each other as individuals with a minimum of such role playing.* Furthermore, these ritualized

---

*The term "role playing" does not imply that the male or female is necessarily consciously "playing a role." As we have mentioned, roles can be so ingrained from countless encounters as to have become an integrated part of that individual's personality and behavioral style.

ways of relating are less prevalent in the higher echelons of the organization. These four role types all limit expressions of competence in women and thus are dysfunctional for success. Males do not experience the reciprocal roles as much of a hindrance. Their roles are evoked only by the presence of women, but women executives almost always work with men and so their roles are more likely to emerge.

More and more women, and to some extent men, are attempting to break these role constraints, but change is slow. For example, it is hard for a woman to keep from being the protected child when her boss treats her as one. She may not be aware of the extent to which he shields her from assignments that are challenging and risky, but which are necessary if she is to develop and advance. Even if she is aware, how can she confront someone who is "only trying to help"?*

In the same way, men often feel confused about how to deal with women. While some females are attempting to change the norms governing interaction between the sexes, there is far from universal agreement by women about how they want to be treated. Males often feel confused about such simple issues as "Should I open the door, help her on with her coat, pick up the tab, or call her Ms.?" Or issues of more substance: "Will she feel I'm patronizing her if I give her some advice about her career?" Relationships have become much more complex, with greater ambiguity about what is expected and what is correct. Like the white liberal who feels helpless when called a racist by a black, so many males feel constrained for fear of being labeled "sexist."

Ironically, the reason men often feel so uncertain about how to relate to women is that they are trapped in traditional sex roles themselves. They are shackled by the social mores of how gentlemen should relate to ladies: protecting them, taking care of them, being responsible for them. Men and women need the freedom to respond to each other as one individual to another.

*One of our female colleagues made the point that she has been held back more by "friends" than by enemies. "With the latter you know where you stand, but with friends they are forever trying to protect you from situations where you might fail."

C. MALE-MALE BONDING:
THE INTERFERENCE OF WOMEN

When men are together, a bonding process develops that does not occur when women are present (Tiger, 1969). The mechanisms are many and varied. For some it can be a discussion of last weekend's football game, cars, or an offhand comment about the physical dimensions of a passing secretary. For others it can be comparing golf scores, or discussing politics and the stock market, or working together on a task. But whatever the subject, the style and tone are such that the message is clear: this is a "man's world." The rapport is perpetuated only so long as the membership is totally male.

Why the change when a female appears? One reason is that these topics serve as one way to assert a traditional definition of masculinity. This form of bonding is based on the exclusion of women. What is shared are interests supposedly not held by women rather than what the members have in common as a result of working on the same project or being employed by the same company. What would happen if a woman in the group were equally knowledgeable and vocal about sports, cars, and politics? If the basis for bonding were solely common interests, then her contributions should be welcome. But isn't it likely that men would feel uncomfortable if a woman corrected them on Monday night's game, knew more about the racing specs of the Porsche, or had a lower handicap? The conversation would soon die out and men would lose the camaraderie that had existed before.

The points raised in the previous section give a clue to another reason why women interfere with the bonding that occurs in an all-male group. The introduction of a woman could activate male-female role relationships so that men would feel great consternation not only about how they should act, but also about what subjects and language are appropriate and inappropriate. The bantering among men often has a veiled competitive tone that attempts to score points without hurting feelings or causing retaliation. Many men feel uncomfortable treating women in a similar fashion or even demonstrating such behavior in front of them. It would be even more threatening if a woman were attractive and fit the Seductress role. This could provoke a different kind of rivalry among the men that would undermine any sense of trust and solidarity among them.

Even when the female is not responded to as the Seductress, concerns about sexuality can interfere with other activities used by men for bonding. Frequently work goes on during lunch and over a drink after five. Not only is work conducted, but people become better acquainted, both crucial in facilitating later business interactions as well as the individual's career development. But men may be hesitant to involve women in such activities. Will luncheon meetings be seen by the woman and coworkers in the same light as if one were to go out with a male peer? Similarly, going out on the town while at conventions or on business trips may not be the same when women are present.

D. THE FEAR OF SEXUAL ENTANGLEMENTS

Sexual liaisons within the same organization, while not unknown, still tend to be negatively sanctioned. Data from the Sex Research Center at the University of Indiana suggest that at least three-fourths of the males in this country commit adultery, but it is not clear how this is spread throughout the management hierarchy. A recent study (Johnson, 1974) reported that only 20 percent of top executives acknowledge having sex outside of marriage. Of these, only one in four indicates involvement on a regular basis; and only 8.8 percent of those, or less than 2 percent of the total sample, reported an affair with a woman in the office. Most of these men go outside of their marriage between the tenth and twentieth years of marriage and are between the ages of thirty-five and forty-five. Regrettably, there are no comparable data on women.

Questions can be raised about whether this sample is representative and whether information were gathered under conditions where the executives would be completely candid. But whatever the actual incidence of office affairs, the fear of their occurrence is very high. Hence the need exists for greater understanding of some of the issues and feelings involved.

Many people with whom we have talked say that when

women and men work together in a noncompetitive relationship, it is only a matter of time before sexual attraction starts to develop. It is doubtful that this occurs in all, or nearly all, cases, but one of the most consistent findings in social psychological research is that contact leads to liking, which in turn leads to more interaction. Two people who work together for some time learn to trust, rely on, and respect each other with a corresponding increase in liking.

Obviously this does not occur in all cases. Knowing another more fully may lead to discovering something we don't like, and working on a project can also be a source of strain and conflict. Also, knowing a man or woman as an equal may remove the mystique and could lead to a rich friendship without sexual involvement.

There are two reasons why it is likely that the incidence of sexual attraction will increase, in addition to the obvious fact that the presence of more women in management raises the number of potential pairs. One is the changing internal structure of contemporary organizations, and the other is the changing cultural norms. As organizations grow more complex with a wide distribution of offices, plants, and clients, travel will increase. The companies that send only males to the field, thus hindering the career opportunities of female executives, may become targets for affirmative action litigation. No longer are women working just eight to five; trips, evening meetings, and conferences set up conditions that make affairs easier to occur.

Societal norms about premarital and extramarital sexuality are changing. While such behavior is not sanctioned by organizations or society, there is greater tolerance for what was once considered highly deviant behavior. Although an affair may still bring great personal pain and can incur costs to job success and reputation, particularly for the female, it is not likely to be as shattering as in the past. Behavior at work cannot be isolated from societal trends, and changes in the culture are likely to be reflected in the office.

Sexual attraction and affairs obviously have their cost, but often overlooked are costs incurred when managers are overly concerned about preventing intimacy from developing. Such vigilance can prevent the emergence of normal relationships. The fear of getting emotionally involved can lead male and female executives to bend over backwards to avoid situations that might appear compromising, like having dinner together or working after hours, but that might increase their task performance. The female can be so worried about appearing seductive that she becomes totally asexual and inhibits all expressions of warmth and caring. The wife at home may be jealous of the female coworker who is able to display skills that the wife has had to submerge. In order to avoid such conflict, the husband may avoid contacts with the female office mate for fear this will cause difficulties at home.

E. WHERE DO WE GO FROM HERE?

The problems we have discussed are complex and deeply rooted in our culture. No easy solutions exist, but as men and women begin to work together to build adult relationships, a first step seems to be to acknowledge the various ways sexuality may be expressed in the office. With this awareness, executives can become sensitive to the possibilities of responses based on sexual stereotypes. They can be more attuned to how men respond to women differentially so that such personally limiting ways of relating can be avoided.

Until recently, consciousness raising has been seen as the domain of women and then of only a few. In several urban areas—Berkeley, Boston, and New York—parallel groups of men have developed to look at the constraints of the male sex role. Such activity has rarely been seen as the concern of organizations. Executives have taken the stance that, at best, participation in such groups is an aspect of personal growth that can be undertaken after hours but it is nothing that business should initiate.

If our analysis is correct, the constraints men and women feel in relating to each other have direct application to work effectiveness. The manager, to be effective, needs to explore to what extent he has been enslaved by sex-role stereotypes, how he feels constrained from arguing with and directly confronting women, how confined he is by traditional definitions of masculinity as seen in films and advertising. The ultimate goal is not one of women's liberation or men's liberation but of human liberation that permits personal development according to individual interests rather than societal sex-role constraints.

For the long run this requires a major shift in cultural mores, but one does not have to wait for societal norms to change before changing the climate in the office. The superior can be very influential in determining what behavior is valued and what is not. Clear signals that competence in women is desired can provide the needed reassurance to the female who is afraid that assertiveness will be seen as unfeminine or castrating. Discouraging the games that men and women play can prevent their continuation.

For such changes to be permanent there must be support throughout the organization. Management development seeks to train executives to better handle technical and administrative aspects of their jobs. Training on the issues we have discussed would be equally useful to increase their awareness of sexism and to develop their ability to more effectively relate to and work with members of the opposite sex.

It is neither possible nor even desirable for people to ignore the sex of one another. At this point in our cultural development it is more desirable to increase awareness so that one can understand how the sex of another is affecting one's behavior. The statement "I want to treat her like I would any other person" is often a veiled form of sexism, for it usually means "like I would any other male." Growing up male or female has had a major impact on the person and how he or she relates to others.

What we are suggesting is that in order for the male executive to understand a woman as an individual, he needs to be aware of how her being a woman has influenced her attitudes and behavior. Equally important, he needs to be aware of how being male has influenced his perceptions and responses to women. Likewise, the woman needs to be aware of how her stereotypes influence her behavior and limit her options in responding to the male executive. What is crucial is that the reality of sexuality as an issue be acknowledged so that men and women in organizations can begin to recognize and explore these issues.

F. SEXUAL ATTRACTION

Increased awareness of the roles that sexuality and sexism play in male-female interaction may help with many of the issues we have discussed but may be less useful in resolving the problem of sexual attraction. If history is any predictor of the future, there may be no simple answer. Troy was not the first, nor last, empire to be lost over sexuality. Each person has to work out his or her own resolution. Some resolve it by working hard to make sure feelings never develop. However, although such a solution prevents the problem from arising, it may have a hidden cost, for to be so concerned and guarded against ever developing attractions can produce a greater than necessary distance and formality. After all, friendship and interpersonal liking are important facilitators in work, be they between the sexes or with the same sex.

Another resolution distinguishes between feelings and behavior. The former need not dictate the latter. People have much more control over their actions than over their emotions. When verbally attacked, it is difficult not to feel anger but easy to refrain from slugging back. So it is with sex. A person can have strong feelings of attraction, and these can continue to exist without leading either to an affair or to disruption of the work relationship.

When feelings of attraction do develop, should they be communicated? In our discussions with managers, no clear outcome emerges. In some situations, sharing of feelings appears to reduce some of the intensity and ambiguity so that individuals can continue to work together and even go out for lunch without fear that intentions will be misinterpreted. Open discussion also allows both people to decide how to deal with their attraction. The attraction then becomes a fact of life and people are free to turn to the task at hand.

For others, such a discussion is uncomfortable; they would much prefer not to acknowledge the attraction. There are no simple answers. What is important is that the issue of sexuality be recognized as a fact of organizational life.

Women in management have been described as a "problem" and an "issue" that must be faced. But equal employment may be the source of greater enrichment for the individual and for the total society as well as for the enlightened organization, and thus any problems encountered may be well worth the price.

REFERENCES

Aries, Elizabeth, "Male-Female Communication in Small Groups," in Alice G. Sargent (ed.), *Beyond Sex Roles*, St. Paul, Minn.: West, in press.

Bakke, E. W., *The Unemployed Man*, New York: Dutton, 1934.

Goldberg, P. A., "Are Women Prejudiced against Women?" *Trans-Action*, April 1968.

Hennig, Margaret, "Family Dynamics and the Successful Woman Executive," in Ruth B. Knudsin (ed.), *Women and Success: The Anatomy of Achievement*, New York: Morrow, 1974.

Horner, Matina, "Femininity and Successful Achievement: A Basic Inconsistency," in Judith Bardwick, Elizabeth Douvan, Matina Horner, and David Guttmann (eds.), *Feminine Personality and Conflict*, Belmont, Calif.: Brooks/Cole, 1970.

Johnson, Harry J., *Executive Life Styles: A Life Extension Institute Report on Alcohol, Sex and Health*, New York: Crowell, 1974.

Kanter, Rosabeth Moss, "Women in Organizations: Change Agent Skills," paper presented at the NTL Conference on New Technology in Organization Development, 1974, published in the conference proceedings.

Korda, Michael, *Male Chauvinism!* New York: Random House, 1972.

Pheterson, G. I., S. B. Kiesler, and P. A. Goldberg, "Evaluation of the Performance of Women as a Function of Their Sex, Achievement, and Personal History," *Journal of Personality and Social Psychology*, vol. 19, no. 1, 1971.

Serbin, Lisa, unpublished doctoral dissertation, Department of Psychology, State University of New York at Stony Brook, 1973; presented at the American Psychological Association, Philadelphia, Spring 1973.

Tiger, Lionel, *Men in Groups*, New York: Random House, 1969.

Chapter IV

The Law:
Where It Is
and Where It's Going

Colquitt L. Meacham

The right to work for a living in the common occupations of the community is of the very essence of the personal freedom and opportunity that it was the purpose of the [Fourteenth] Amendment to secure.

Truax v. Raich, 239 U.S. 33, 41 (1915)

Ten years ago, when the Civil Rights Act of 1964 was being hotly debated in Congress, very little attention was given to the issue of sex discrimination. Indeed concern was so minor that coverage for women under the act was not originally planned or contemplated by its proponents. At the last minute—the day before the House of Representatives voted on the act—Representative Howard Smith added sex as a protected category to Title VII of the statute. It is generally believed that Smith's action was not motivated by concern for women workers, but rather was designed to torpedo the entire statute. The assumption was that legislators willing to give protection to racial minorities would balk at the absurd proposition of extending such equality of treatment to women and that passage of the act would be

SEX DISCRIMINATION IN EMPLOYMENT

	Title VII of the Civil Rights Act of 1964 as amended by the Equal Opportunity Act of 1972.	Executive Order 11246 as amended by 11375.	Equal Pay Act of 1963 as amended by Education Amendments of 1972 (Higher Education Act).
WHO IS COVERED?	All institutions with 15 or more employees.	All institutions with federal contracts of over $10,000.	Industries engaged in interstate commerce. Employees covered by Fair Labor Standards Act.
WHAT IS PROHIBITED?	Discrimination in employment (including hiring, upgrading, salaries, fringe benefits, training and other conditions of employment) on the basis of race, color, religion, national origin, or sex.	Discrimination in employment (including hiring, upgrading, salaries, fringe benefits, training and other conditions of employment) on the basis of race, religion, national origin, or sex.	Discrimination in salaries (including almost all fringe benefits) on the basis of sex.
EXEMPTIONS FROM COVERAGE	Religious institutions are exempt with respect to employment of individuals of a particular religion or religious order.	Non-federal contractors and employees. Non-federally assisted construction.	Local, state and federal governments. Industries exempted from Fair Labor Standards Act.
WHO ENFORCES THE PROVISIONS?	Equal Employment Opportunity Commission (EEOC)	Office of Federal Contract Compliance (OFCC) of the Department of Labor has policy responsibility and oversees federal agency enforcement programs.	Wage and Hour Division of the Employment Standards Administration of the Department of Labor.
CAN THE ENTIRE INSTITUTION BE REVIEWED?	Yes. EEOC may investigate part or all of an establishment.	Yes. Contracting agency may investigate part or all of an institution.	Yes. Usually the Wage and Hour Division reviews the entire establishment.
RECORD KEEPING	Institution must keep and preserve specified records relevant to the determination of whether violations have		

	Title VII of the Civil Rights Act of 1964 as amended by the Equal Opportunity Act of 1972.	Executive Order 11246 as amended by 11375.	Equal Pay Act of 1963 as amended by Education Amendments of 1972 (Higher Education Act).
ENFORCEMENT POWER AND SANCTIONS	If attempts at conciliation fail, EEOC or the U.S. Attorney General may file suit. Aggrieved individuals may also initiate suits. Court may enjoin respondent from engaging in unlawful behavior, order appropriate affirmative action, order reinstatement and award back pay.	Government may delay new contracts, revoke current contracts, and disqualify institutions from eligibility for future contracts.	If voluntary compliance fails Secretary of Labor may file suit. Aggrieved individuals may initiate suits when Department of Labor has not done so. Court may enjoin respondent from engaging in unlawful behavior, and order salary raises, back pay and interest.
AFFIRMATIVE ACTION REQUIREMENTS	Affirmative Action is not required unless charges have been filed, in which case it may be included in the conciliation agreement or be ordered by court.	Affirmative Action plans (including numerical goals and timetables) are required of all contractors with contracts of $50,000 or more and 50 or more employees.	Affirmative Action, other than salary increases and back pay, is not required.
COVERAGE OF LABOR ORGANIZATIONS	Labor organizations are covered by the same requirements and sanctions as employers.	Any agreement a contractor may have with a labor organization cannot be in conflict with the contractor's affirmative action commitment.	Labor organizations are prohibited from causing or attempting to cause an employer to discriminate on the basis of sex. Suits may be brought against these organizations.
IS HARASSMENT PROHIBITED?	Institutions are prohibited from discharging or discriminating against any employee or applicant for employment because she/he has made a complaint, assisted with an investigation, or instituted proceedings.		

defeated. Smith's plan backfired, and the bill passed the House and Senate with the sex provision of Title VII, the only title to mention sex, receiving very little attention.

The year before passage of the Civil Rights Act, the Fair Labor Standards Act of 1938 was amended by the Equal Pay Act,[1] which guaranteed to women equal pay for work equal to that of male employees. Unlike the Civil Rights Act, the Equal Pay Act was passed by Congress after hearings establishing the fact that wage discrimination on the basis of sex was widespread. Representative Donahue, commenting on why the legislation was necessary, said, "This measure represents the correction of basic injustice being visited upon women in many fields of endeavor . . . extending simple wage justice to the increasing corps of America's working women."[2] In addition to these federal statutes more than half the states have by now legislated bans on sex discrimination in employment.[3]

A. LEGISLATIVE ACTION

The passage of Title VII and the Equal Pay Act, coupled with the growing consciousness of women in our society, has resulted in progress toward equality for working women that few would have predicted. Complaints filed under the Equal Pay Act have resulted so far in businesses paying out $43 million to 104,000 employees over a ten-year period.[4] Most of these complaints have been settled without litigation, and of the approximately 400 lawsuits filed, most have been decided in favor of the female complainant.[5]

The Equal Employment Opportunity Commission (hereafter referred to as the EEOC) has responsibility for enforcing Title VII of the Civil Rights Act, and reports that approximately one-third of its complaints involve sex discrimination. Many of these complaints have resulted in litigation, and the first Title VII case to reach the United States Supreme Court involved sex discrimination.[6]

The judicial decisions under Title VII have generally been very favorable to the women plaintiffs. The procedural aspects of the statute have been construed broadly, in favor of the plaintiffs,[7] and the exceptions have been construed narrowly so as to defeat defendant employers' defenses.[8]

1. Recent Amendments

In 1972 important amendments were made to both Title VII and the Equal Pay Act. Coverage under the Equal Pay Act has now been extended to executive, administrative, professional, and outside sales employees.[9] This means that women working in such jobs must receive salaries equal to men performing the same duties. All employers are to review the salaries of women working in these categories, women in supervisory and administrative jobs high in the corporate structure, to make sure that pay is commensurate with that of male employees. The jobs of the women and men need not be identical, but only substantially equal as to skill, effort, responsibility, and working conditions. Attempts to disguise the similarity of two jobs by giving them different titles, or by assigning the men insignificant additional tasks, will not be allowed.[10]

For example, the female employees of a bank sued under the Equal Pay Act alleging that they were being paid substantially lower wages than male employees doing the same work. The bank responded by explaining that the men were in a training program that qualified the higher pay. The court found, from evidence presented, that the training program was little more than a hastily devised justification for the unequal pay. The program, if it in fact existed, was informal, sporadic, and unwritten. The training was essentially the acquiring of skills and knowledge of the business through performance of regular tasks also performed by women and was not a valid basis for the wage difference.[11]

2. The Equal Employment Opportunity Commission

The most important and controversial aspect of the amendments was granting to the EEOC the power to initiate court action against an employer.[12] Formerly the EEOC had no enforcement power and could merely seek voluntary compliance from employers through conciliation. Under the old law only the complainant could file suit in federal court to litigate the question of discrimination. Lack of enforcement power crippled the EEOC in the past and made it relatively ineffective. Now, with its new enforcement powers and a staff of attorneys at litigation offices throughout the country, the EEOC has begun to take a strong role in prosecuting evasive employers.

In the past, employers could engage in various dilatory tactics when dealing with a Title VII action, hoping the complainant would get discouraged at the prospect of finding a lawyer and filing suit and would eventually give up. Employers failed to take the EEOC conciliation procedure seriously because they knew the EEOC could do nothing if they failed to cooperate. This attitude has undoubtedly begun to change now, and employers are well advised to settle a complaint at the conciliation stage if possible, for a lawsuit against the EEOC could be costly.

An example of what the EEOC can now achieve is the settlement it made with AT&T in January 1973. AT&T agreed to pay approximately $15 million to 13,000 women and 2,000 minority men who had been denied pay and promotion opportunities. New policies agreed on by the company and EEOC should result in increased wages of $23 million a year.

The consent decree entered in the AT&T case includes a detailed affirmative action plan that requires the company to evaluate women in its management training program for promotion. The criteria employed in making the evaluations must be approved by the EEOC and women found satisfactory are to become candidates for promotion as vacancies occur. Additionally, those found satisfactory are to receive a salary increase of $100 a month as of the assessment date.[13]

B. ADMINISTRATIVE AND JUDICIAL DECISIONS

1. Job Requirements

The second Title VII case to be decided by the United States Supreme Court, *Griggs v. Duke Power Co.*,[14] involved racial discrimination, but the principles articulated by the Court are equally applicable to cases involving sex discrimination.

The plaintiffs in the *Griggs* case were challenging Duke Power Company's practice of requiring an employee or job applicant to be a high school graduate or pass an intelligence test as a condition of employment or promotion. The requirement, though applied equally to whites and blacks, excluded a disproportionate number of blacks from eligibility.

The Court found that the intelligence tests and high school education did not bear a demonstrable relationship to the successful performance of the jobs for which they were used and were therefore not necessary for the employer's business. Because of their discriminatory impact on blacks, the tests were therefore in violation of Title VII.

In its opinion the Court said, "Good intent or absence of discriminatory intent does not redeem employment procedures or testing mechanisms that operate as 'built in headwinds' for minority groups and are unrelated to measuring job capability."[15]

The decision requires employers to take a close look at job descriptions and qualifications. If they contain irrelevant requirements that disproportionately exclude women, they are illegal, and should be revised to include only qualifications essential to performance of the job.

2. The "Bona Fide Occupational Qualification" Exception

Under Title VII, valid business necessity can excuse practices that are discriminatory in instances where religion, sex, or national origin is "a bona fide occupational qualification reasonably necessary to the normal operation of that particular business or enterprise. . . ."[16]

This is the famous "b.f.o.q." exception that employers seized upon after the passage of Title VII to justify their discriminatory practices. These attempts, however, have been thwarted by a narrow interpretation of the b.f.o.q. by EEOC and the courts.

In its *Guidelines on Sex Discrimination*,[17] the EEOC has stated that the following situations do not warrant application of the b.f.o.q. exception: (1) the refusal to hire a woman because of her sex based on assumptions about the comparative employment characteristics of women in general; (2) the refusal to hire an individual based on stereotyped characterization of the sexes; (3) the refusal to hire an individual because of the preferences of coworkers, the employer, clients, or customers. In fact, the EEOC has limited the b.f.o.q. for use only "where it is necessary for the purpose of authenticity or genuineness, . . . e.g., an actor or actress."[18] The EEOC *Guidelines* do not have the effect of law, but the courts have conceded to them great deference as a valid interpretation of the will of Congress.[19]

In most cases where defendants attempted to use the b.f.o.q. defense, the courts have followed the example of the EEOC and given the exception a narrow interpretation. Probably the most famous of these cases is *Diaz v. Pan American World Airways*,[20] in which the male plaintiffs challenged Pan Am's policy of hiring only females as flight cabin attendants.

Pan Am attempted to justify this policy by proof that sex was a "bona fide occupational qualification" for the position of stewardess. The court observed:

> Reviewing its own experience with the thousands of male and female cabin attendants it had hired over the preceding years, Pan Am determined in 1959 that the overall level of service provided by the females it had hired was superior to that provided by the males it had hired. While the males were found capable of satisfactorily performing what Pan Am describes as the "mechanical" functions of the flight attendant's job, such as the storage of coats and the preparation and service of meals and beverages, the male stewards were found, as a group, not to be the equal of the females in the "nonmechanical" functions which had now become more important—providing reassurance to anxious passengers, giving courteous personalized service, and in general, making flights as pleasurable as possible within the limitations imposed by aircraft operation.[21]

Evidence that their passengers overwhelmingly preferred service by females included an Opinion Research Corporation survey commissioned by the airline which showed that 79 percent of the passengers questioned preferred female stewardesses. The noted psychiatrist Dr. Eric Berne testified in psychological terms as to why passengers of both sexes prefer female stewardesses. The District Court was convinced by Pan Am's evidence and ruled that sex was a b.f.o.q. for position of flight attendant and denied the males relief.[22]

The Court of Appeals for the Fifth Circuit, however, reversed the District Court and held that sex was not a b.f.o.q. for the cabin attendant position. In its opinion the court adopted the EEOC *Guidelines* that require a narrow interpretation of the b.f.o.q. exception. In ruling that men as well as women must be considered for the jobs, the court said, "The primary function of an airline is to transport passengers safely from one point to another. While a pleasant environment, enhanced by the obvious cosmetic effect that female stewardesses provide as well as . . . their apparent ability to perform the non-mechanical functions of the job in a more effective manner than most men, may all be important, they are tangential to the essence of the business involved."[23]

Employers have frequently tried to justify their reluctance to promote women to management positions with arguments centered on customer or coworker preference. The assertion that clients do not want to have a female working on their account or that male employees do not want a female supervisor is not a legitimate defense for the employer. The Pan American case seems to have settled that question once and for all.

3. Fringe Benefits

Another area of sex discrimination, less widely discussed at first than the b.f.o.q. exemption, is the question of fringe benefits. Until recently employers felt justified in giving females lower fringe benefits on the assumption that most women work for a second family income or as a hobby, and are covered by their husbands' benefits.

In its *Guidelines*, the EEOC has defined as fringe benefits medical, hospital, accident, life insurance, and retirement benefits; profit-sharing and bonus plans; leave; and other terms, conditions, and privileges of employment.[24] According to the EEOC, it is an unlawful practice for an employer to discriminate between men and women with regard to fringe benefits by such distinctions as conditioning benefits on whether the employee is the "head of the household," or "principal wage earner;" giving benefits to the families of male employees but not to families of female employees; or having a pension or retirement plan that establishes different optional or compulsory retirement ages or benefits for men and women.[25]

As yet there has been very little litigation in this area, perhaps because most unions bargain for benefits plans that treat men and women equally. Employers should review their fringe benefit plans carefully to be sure men and women are receiving equal benefits. They are advised to revise discriminatory policies even if it means reopening a union contract. If the union refuses to cooperate, the employer can make the union a codefendant should a complaint or lawsuit be filed.

One case that reached the Court of Appeals for the Seventh Circuit[26] involved a retirement plan adopted pursuant to a collective bargaining agreement, in which it was agreed that women were to retire at sixty-two, men at sixty-five. The court found that the plan violated Title VII because it forced women to give up three years of work and wages, based on a sexual classification contrary to the intent of Title VII.

Because insurance companies who set up benefit programs rely on actuarial tables, they write plans that give men a larger annuity than women because women as a group live longer than men. The controversy over the use of actuarial tables will undoubtedly not be easily settled, but some questions must be asked about the accuracy of actuarial figures. Do working women as a group outlive working men? Many of the tables were compiled when fewer women were working. Are there regional variations in life expectancy? Why use sex when smoking or weight is far more relevant to life expectancy? This application of a stereotyped characteristic to individual workers is in direct contradiction to Title VII's directive that individuals be treated as such, and not as members of a sexual group.

Another recent case appears, at least implicitly, to reject actuarial figures as a legitimate basis for discriminating against men or women as a group under retirement plans. In *Rosen v. Public Service Electric Co.*[27] the court ruled that retirement benefits must be equal for men and women of like ages possessing comparable work experience. Where there were disparities, the company was required to raise the benefits of the group discriminated against.

4. Maternity Benefits

Probably the most troublesome problem for a woman who has decided she wants children and a career is how to arrange her pregnancies and child rearing to accommodate her job responsibilities. A satisfactory solution to these problems is critical if women are to enter and remain in managerial positions. These are the alternatives:

> If her employment is terminated or suspended with a loss of accumulated benefits [during pregnancy], her incentive to return to work is correspondingly reduced. If the woman who worked prior to motherhood waits until after her children are grown to re-enter the labor force, she becomes the victim of discrimination on the basis of her age as well as her sex. But if she can be reinstated after absence required by childbirth with no loss of benefits, she is more likely to view employment as a career in which she has a vested interest, rather than as a mere temporary source of income, and will arrange her pregnancies so as to disrupt her employment activity as little as possible.[28]

How employers treat pregnancy and what types of benefits are provided for female employees will profoundly affect many women's careers, especially their ability to progress to management positions.

Maternity benefits include job security, maintenance of accrued seniority and continuation of its accrual during pregnancy leave, eligibility for temporary disability compensation. continued membership in health and life insurance plans, and adequate maternity leave. Maternity leave should be distinguished from child-care leave. Only women employees require maternity leave for childbirth, generally not more than six weeks. Leave to take care of the child, however, should be treated differently from maternity leave and should be available to both male and female employees.

Concern for the health of the pregnant woman and her

unborn child is often cited as the reason for extended maternity leave. This fails to recognize that many pregnant women care for small children and perform strenuous housekeeping duties up to the date of birth. Another common argument is that pregnant women do not work efficiently. While some pregnant women may have difficulties, this does not mean that all or even most women will be unfit to perform their jobs. Annual Public Health Service surveys show that men lose about the same amount of time from work because of disabilities as women, even including childbirth and the complications of pregnancy.[29]

The United States Supreme Court has recently spoken for the first time on the question of mandatory maternity leave. At the time the lawsuits were filed, local governments were not covered by Title VII, and so plaintiffs alleged violations of their constitutional rights under the Fourteenth Amendment. The two cases involved maternity regulations of the Cleveland, Ohio, Board.[30] The Cleveland regulation required pregnant teachers to stop work five months before the expected date of birth and remain out without pay until the first semester after the baby reaches three months of age. The Chesterfield regulation required the teacher to take leave without pay four months before the expected birth, but she could return when her doctor certified she was able to work.

The Supreme Court struck down both regulations, stating, "The rules contain an irrebuttable presumption of physical incompetency, and that presumption applies even when the medical evidence as to an individual woman's physical status might be wholly to the contrary. [Such] . . . permanent irrebuttable presumptions have long been disfavored under the Due Process Clauses of the Fifth and Fourteenth Amendments."[31] The Court stressed that "freedom of personal choice in matters of marriage and family life is one of the liberties protected by the Due Process Clause of the Fourteenth Amendment. By acting to penalize the pregnant teacher for deciding to bear a child, overly restrictive maternity leave regulations can constitute a heavy burden on the exercise of these protected freedoms."[32]

In a footnote, the Court conceded that the alternative of an individualized determination could be an administrative burden to the employer, and indicated that a more narrowly drawn regulation, requiring maternity leave during the last few weeks of pregnancy, might be permissible. In its most narrow interpretation, this decision says that mandatory maternity leaves may not be arbitrary and capricious and based on irrebuttable presumptions that have no basis in fact.

Another aspect of maternity provisions was considered when in June 1974 the United States Supreme Court ruled in *Geduldig v. Aiello*[33] that California's exclusion of normal pregnancy and childbirth from coverage under its statewide disability insurance program does not constitute "invidious" discrimination and therefore is constitutional under the Equal Protection Clause of the Fourteenth Amendment. The Court said the state had a legitimate interest in keeping the program self-supporting, in minimizing the employee contribution rate, and in keeping benefits for covered disabilities at an adequate level.

It is important to note that *Geduldig v. Aiello* involved the actions of legislators, not employers, and was decided pursuant to the Fourteenth Amendment, not Title VII of the Civil Rights Act. The EEOC has stated in its *Guidelines* that Title VII requires pregnant employees to be treated on the same basis as any other employee with a temporary disability under a health or sick leave plan available to employees.[34]

In its "Friend of the Court" brief filed in the *Geduldig* case the EEOC stated that

> The Commission carefully scrutinized both the employer practices and their crucial impact on women for a substantial period of time and then issued its Guidelines after it became increasingly apparent that symptomatic or pervasive discrimination against women was frequently found in employers' denial of employment opportunity and benefits to women on the basis of the childbearing role, performed solely by women.[35]

Several lower federal courts have considered the "pregnancy as temporary disability" issue in cases filed under Title VII, and have ruled that discriminatory treatment of pregnant employees under health insurance plans violates the act.[36]

In light of the administrative and judicial rulings, what type of maternity leave program should an employer adopt? For the women who want to work as long as possible and take as little time off for childbirth as is physically necessary, short-term disability insurance should be available. If benefits and seniority accrue during leave for other disabilities, they should accrue during such maternity leave. If accumulated sick pay must be exhausted before disability benefits are paid, then pregnant women could so use their sick pay. A woman who wants to leave work in the early months of her pregnancy, although she is physically capable of continuing her job, clearly should not be entitled to disability compensation, but such voluntary leave might be treated in the same manner as educational leave so that these women retain seniority and receive preference in hiring when they are ready to return.[37]

In a society where many families have both parents working but child care is woefully inadequate, it is essential for both parents to have the flexibility to take voluntary leaves for child care. Voluntary leave to care for children should be available to fathers as well as mothers. Such leaves would provide no benefits, but would freeze the employees' seniority and assure them a job, though possibly not the same job, when they return to work.

C. FUTURE DEVELOPMENTS

1. Punitive Damages

In October 1973, a Federal District Court in Michigan found that Detroit Edison had discriminated against employees on the basis of race, and ordered them to pay $4 million in punitive damages, in addition to back pay.[38] The court found that Detroit Edison's conduct had been so unreasonable that it constituted malice, which made the award of punitive damages appropriate and necessary. If this decision is affirmed on appeal and followed by other courts, it will give employees tremendous leverage in such cases.

It is not at all clear that Title VII empowers courts to award punitive damages. Such an order may well violate the employer's constitutional right to due process, since the act does not provide for a jury trial in such cases. What this case indicates is that an employer's conduct must be unusually outrageous to make punitive damages appropriate.

2. The Bank of America Settlement

In July 1974, a federal judge in San Francisco signed a consent decree involving the Bank of America and its female employees. The decree sets forth the obligation of the bank to develop, over a three-year period, four trust funds, totaling $3.75 million, to benefit women bank employees. These trust funds are to be used by women employees for self-development or training. Significantly, the largest of the four trusts ($1.9 million) is the Management Training Trust. The potential beneficiaries of this trust are women college graduates employed by the bank who have not been placed in management training programs.

The court also established goals and timetables for the participation of women in management training programs (including overseas training programs) and for the employment of women as ranking branch officers.

The trust and employment goals and timetables were accepted by the plaintiffs in the bank case in lieu of back pay. This innovative and practical solution to management development, providing both the incentive and the means to move women into executive positions, may well become a pattern for future settlements in sex discrimination cases.

3. The Equal Rights Amendment

Thirty-three of the thirty-eight states necessary have ratified the Equal Rights Amendment to the United States Constitution. The amendment reads as follows, "Equality of rights under the law shall not be denied or abridged by the United States or by any State on account of sex." This means that the law may in no way treat men and women differently because of their sex. Any classification based on sex will be illegal. Passage of the amendment will not mean drastic changes for employers because sex discrimination in employment has already been outlawed by the federal laws noted above and by many state laws. The b.f.o.q. in

Title VII would be illegal under the Equal Rights Amendment, but as a practical matter, since the b.f.o.q. has been interpreted so narrowly, the change would mean very little.

The major impact the Equal Rights Amendment would have on employment involves protective labor laws still in effect in some states. These laws are of three types: (1) laws that confer benefit on one sex or the other, such as required rest periods for women but not men; (2) laws that exclude women from certain occupations or from employment under certain circumstances; (3) laws that restrict conditions of employment for women, such as maximum hours, night work, and weight-lifting limits.

The invalidation of all these state laws by the Equal Rights Amendment has become a matter of great concern to many working women, who fear employers will deprive them of benefits provided by such laws. While this might happen, it is also possible that the result will be to extend benefits such as minimum wage and rest periods to men, thereby treating the sexes equally and complying with the amendment.

During the two years after ratification before the amendment takes effect, it will be necessary to screen existing legislation and discard laws that are discriminatory, such as those excluding women from certain occupations, and to amend laws benefiting only one sex so that all employees, male and female, are protected equally.

The importance of the amendment is suggested by the observation that

> The adoption of a constitutional amendment will also have effects that go far beyond the legal system. The demand for equality of rights before the law is only a part of a broader claim by women for the elimination of rigid sex role determinism. And this in turn is part of a more general movement for the recognition of individual potential, the development of new sets of relationships between individuals and groups, and the establishment of institutions which will promote the values and respect the sensibilities of all persons. Adoption of an Equal Rights Amendment would be a sign that the nation is prepared to accept and support new creative forces that are stirring in our society.[39]

The momentum has been generated and some laws have been passed, but complete equality for women is yet to be realized. While many of the blatant discriminatory practices have disappeared, subtle barriers still remain. We have laws, but most women still work in low-paying, low-status jobs, and only a few find their way to the more prestigious positions. The successful woman is still a news item—something unusual—and the stereotypes about women persist. Only when women represent significant percentages of executives, professionals, and high government officials will we have achieved real equality.

NOTES

1 29 U.S.C. 206(d).
2 109 Cong. Rec. 9212.
3 All laws and regulations dealing with sex discrimination in employment can be found in the *Employment Practices Guide*, published by the Commerce Clearing House, Inc., or *Fair Employment Manual*, published by the Bureau of National Affairs.
4 Burns, *Analysis of the Equal Pay Act*, 24 Lab. L. J. 92 (1973).
5 *Business Week*, Nov. 25, 1972.
6 *Phillips v. Martin Marietta Corp.*, 400 U.S. 542 (1971).
7 *Bowe v. Colgate-Palmolive Co.*, 416 F. 2d 711, 718 (7th Cir. 1969).
8 *Diaz v. Pan American World Airways*, 442 F. 2d 385 (5th Cir. 1971), *Sprogis v. United Air Lines Inc.*, 442 F.2d 1194 (7th Cir. 1971), cert. denied 404 U.S. 991.
9 Pub. L. 92-318, Title IX §906(b)(1), 86 Stat. 375 (June 23, 1972).
10 *Shultz v. Wheaton Glass Co.*, 421 F. 2d 259 (3d Cir. 1970), cert. denied 398 U.S. 905.
11 *Hodgson v. American Bank of Commerce*, 447 F. 2d 416 (5th Cir. 1971).
12 Pub. L. 92-261.
13 FEP 431:73.
14 401 U.S. 424 (1971).
15 Id. at 432.
16 42 U.S.C. §2000e-2(e).
17 29 C.F.R. §1604.1-1604.31.
18 Id. §1604.2 (a)(z).
19 *Griggs v. Duke Power Co.*, 401 U.S. 424, 434 (1971).

20   443 F. 2d 385 (5th Cir. 1971).

21   *Diaz v. Pan American World Airways*, 311 F. Supp. 559, 563 (1970).

22   Id.

23   *Diaz*, op. cit. supra note 21, at 388.

24   29 C.F.R. 1604.9(a).

25   Id.

26   *Bartmess v. Drewrys U.S.A. Inc.*, 444 F. 2d 1186 (7th Cir.), cert. denied, 404 U.S. 939 (1971).

27   477 F. 2d 90 (3d Cir. 1973).

28   *Love's Labors Lost: New Conceptions of Maternity Leaves*, 7 Harv. Civ. Rights–Civ. Lib. L. Rev. 260, 261 (1972).

29   U.S. Public Health Service, Dept. of Health, Education and Welfare, Pub. 1000, Ser. 10, No. 52, *Vital and Health Statistics, Current Estimates from the Health Interview Survey*, U.S., 1967.

30   *Cleveland Board of Education v. La Fleur*, 94 S. Ct. 791 (1974); *Cohen v. Chesterfield County School Board*, 94 S. Ct. 791 (1974).

31   Id. at 798.

32   Id. at 796.

33   94 S. Ct. 2485 (1974).

34   29 C.F.R. §1604.10(b).

35   *Geduldig v. Aiello*, 94 S. Ct. 2485, 2494 (1974).

36   *Wetzel v. Liberty Mutual Ins. Co.*, 372 F. Supp. 1146 (W.D. Pa. 1974).

37   *Love's Labors Lost*, supra, note 28, at 291.

38   *Stamps v. Detroit Edison Co.*, 365 F. Supp. 87 (E.D. Mich. 1973).

39   Brown, *The Equal Rights Amendment: A Constitutional Basis for Equal Rights for Women*, 80 Yale L. Rev. 871, 885 (1971).

Chapter V

Bringing Women into Management: Basic Strategies

Myra H. Strober

The basic question we shall be discussing in this chapter is *how* to bring women into management. But before we consider the "how" question in detail, we must address the question of *why* companies should be interested in bringing women into management, for the "why" question is closely related to the "how" question.

Apart from the moral issues, the two basic answers to the "why" question involve money. The first reason for bringing women into management is to avoid trouble: i.e., to avoid costly lawsuits, to avoid the possible cancellation or loss of government contracts, and to avoid unfavorable publicity. These motivations are certainly not unimportant. In fact, it is probably correct to assume that without governmental and court sanctions or potential sanctions very little would be happening today to bring women into management.

But the second reason for bringing women into management

is at least as important: namely, that there are tremendous opportunity costs involved in the underutilization of women. And it is crucial when designing an affirmative action program for women that companies recognize these opportunity costs.

A company that brings women into management only in order to comply with governmental requirements may be inclined to operate only a token affirmative action program. A program designed merely to avoid trouble, however, misses the opportunity to utilize a critical source of untapped ideas and talents. And a program that waits to be pushed into action by a lawsuit runs a particularly high risk of rejection by fellow employees. People work far more sincerely to bring about affirmative action when they help to design the program than when they feel the program is being forced upon them by some outside agency. Thus the "how" question that should interest companies is not "How do I do as little as possible?" but rather "How do I effectively utilize untapped talent?" "How do I successfully bring in large numbers of new women managers?"

Bringing in large numbers of women is not costless. Many of these proposals are costly—in terms of executive time and corporate money. But while these costs exist, they are outweighed by benefits both to the company and to the society as a whole: the benefits of avoiding trouble and the benefits of increasing the corporate managerial talent pool.

Given these justifications, let us consider how best to proceed. To solve the problem of the underrepresentation of women in management, it is necessary to move forward simultaneously with two types of strategies—a short-run strategy and a long-run strategy. The short-run strategy is designed primarily to provide direct benefits, to produce relatively rapid results that meet the organization's immediate requirements. The long-run strategy, on the other hand, while having some immediate impact, is designed primarily to provide derivative benefits, to bring about gradual, more complex changes in people's perceptions about women and their role in business and society. Let us look first at the short-run strategy for bringing women into management.

A. STRATEGIES FOR DIRECT BENEFITS

Epstein, in Chapter I, has already described the institutional barriers that make it so difficult for women to achieve high managerial positions. In the short run, breaking down these barriers requires increased attention to four areas: the encouragement of women employees; the improvement, among employees, of interpersonal communication between the sexes; the modification of employee search procedures; and the modification of job design.

1. Encouragement of Women

The encouragement of women is a crucial part of the short-run strategy. Because most of today's women have been socialized to believe that management, like fatherhood, is for men, women who aspire to managerial careers need frequent reinforcement of their aspirations. Some evidence on the importance of encouragement may be seen in some recent data from the University of California.[1] Women who began their graduate studies at Berkeley in 1962 dropped out of graduate school at a considerably higher rate than did their male counterparts. But recently, the University Affirmative Action Office and the Campus Center for Continuing Education of Women sponsored a pilot project of encouragement for women graduate students. Weekly sessions were held at which women from diverse fields of study met to talk about their mutual concerns. As a result of this project, and probably as a result of the women's movement and the increase in women faculty—both of which also provide encouragement for women students—the dropout rate for women graduate students at Berkeley has declined sharply. For the group that began graduate studies in 1968, the dropout rate for women was equal to the rate for men.

Encouragement for women requires opening channels of communication among women already in the company. Through talking with peers and meeting older women who serve as role models, women increase their self-confidence, learn to deal with their frequent sense of isolation, and develop new tools for

dealing with their problems. The importance of role models cannot be stressed enough. When a young woman sees that another
woman has "made it" in her company—when she sees that it's
possible to make it—her aspirations are tremendously enhanced.
Female peers are important to women too. If you're bringing in
women managers, try to bring in more than one. Two or three
women can help to encourage one another. Then, too, if one
woman fails, at least there are some others around so that failure
isn't attributed to women as a group.

Encouragement also requires good career counseling. It
requires teaching men, who at the present time are generally the
ones involved in performance reviews, how to motivate women
managers and how to help women to recognize and attain their
goals. Men need to be taught how to encourage women and, in
particular, how to provide honest negative and positive feedback.
Many male managers frequently experience awkwardness in
counseling their female subordinates. In such cases, they need to
be made more cognizant of their own difficulties and of their
subordinates' desires to be treated honestly. If a woman is doing
something incorrectly, she must find out what to do differently.
Men who "try to be nice" without being honest simply deal a
deathblow to a woman's career development.

Finally, men who do career counseling for women need to be
made aware of a typical career pitfall for women. Women in
management frequently become trapped in staff specialist positions, i.e., staff specialization; they don't get the general management experience—the line experience—they need.[2] Good career
counseling must include pointing out the disadvantages of specialization and giving women the support and encouragement
they may need to broaden their experience.

2. Improvement of Interpersonal Communication Skills between Men and Women

The second part of the short-run strategy involves the improvement of interpersonal communication skills between the sexes.
Many of the barriers described arise because men and women do
not yet know how to interact as competitors or as colleagues.

Additional difficulties often occur in situations where women supervise men.

As Theodore Capwell points out in his book *The Sociology of Work*,[3] boys are educated from early childhood regarding the "severe prohibition of fighting with girls." This generalizes later on to a prohibition of competition between the sexes. As Bradford, Sargent, and Sprague point out (in Chapter III), adolescent and college women who persist in competing with men usually do so at the expense of their popularity or social life. Not many adults today have had the experience of working in a situation where men and women are colleagues, companions, professional acquaintances, or friends. Men and women have learned to relate to one another as sexual partners or potential sexual partners. They have also learned to relate to one another in certain traditional occupational or social situations, for example as doctor-nurse or boss-secretary or wife–husband's friend. But most men find it difficult to completely dismiss the potential-sexual-partner model from their minds when they are asked to deal with women as equals. There are many who feel that since women are usually assumed to hold lower-prestige jobs, welcoming women as equals into a profession can only serve to downgrade the profession.

Because the roots of the problem are so deep, in the short run the corporation probably can hope to do no more than remove the most serious manifestations. But corporate managers should understand that modifying their usual behavior may be necessary and that the development of appropriate working relationships with persons of the opposite sex is considered an important part of every individual's job. Open discussion of the tensions between the sexes can help to pinpoint the difficulties at a conscious level and may itself help to change outward behavior. In other cases, particular solutions may be worked out by the group. Some professional women find, for example, that men are more comfortable in treating them as colleagues once the women have also established their identity as wives. Seeing women colleagues as wives seems to lessen the men's anxiety or uncertainty or guilt about developing a work rapport. Husbands and wives of employees surely must be made part of any attempt to change working relationships between men and women.

One particularly awkward interpersonal relationship is that of female supervisor and male subordinate. As many anthropologists have noted,[4] in societies where women raise children, young men establish their maleness by breaking away from female domination. As a result, some young men find their manhood threatened when they are required to "take orders" from a woman manager. Significantly, a *Harvard Business Review* survey of male manager attitudes several years ago found that "acceptance of women in managerial roles appears to increase with the age of the man . . . with the big change occurring at age 40."[5] Although the corporation cannot deal with the origin of the domination problem, open discussion should prove helpful if managers know that dealing with the issue is required. Perhaps most important is learning by doing. It is interesting to reflect on the *Harvard Business Review*'s report that men who have actually worked with women are more likely to favor placing women in managerial positions.[6]

3. Modification of Employee Search Procedures

The third element in this short-run strategy involves the modification of employee search procedures. The basic reason for suggesting modifications in employee search procedures is that current procedures tend to overlook potential talent.

The waste of female managerial talent has two dimensions. One is the misallocation of resources, decrease in productivity, and increase in turnover that come about through failure to promote women already in the organization. The second aspect of this waste is the failure to utilize women not presently in the business sector of the economy.

The slow or nonexistent promotion process for women means that in many jobs women not only incompletely utilize their skills but also have very little incentive to perform at high levels. A recent study at the University of Michigan sheds some interesting light on this point.[7] The study, based on interviews with about 1,500 workers, showed that people's attitudes toward promotion were strongly tied to their expectations of being promoted. Women aspire to promotion and work hard to achieve it when they believe that their chances of achieving it are pretty good. Motivation to strive hard requires a hospitable soil. Companies should look for potential talent among all female employees.

Job openings should be posted so that qualified women may make their interest in promotion known. And the personnel department should take an active role in maintaining up-to-date files of women employees' interests and qualifications so that the department can encourage particular candidates to apply for available jobs. Legally speaking, as a result of Revised Order 4,[8] the employer's obligation has gone well past the necessity to merely post job openings. Companies interested in making a sincere effort to increase the number of women in previously all-male or virtually all-male jobs must make personal, aggressive efforts to get women to apply. After years of exclusion, women may not be convinced that just because a company posts a job that the company really means, to paraphrase the military, that Uncle Sam wants women.

A slow or nonexistent promotion process is also costly in terms of increased turnover. A young man who fails to get his expected promotion frequently transfers to another company or industry where he can better his chances. The same is true for a young woman.

The question of relative turnover rates for men and women is an important one. In fact, many have claimed that because women have higher turnover rates than men, the exclusion of women from management should not be considered discrimination, but rather sensible economic judgment. The difficulty with comparing turnover rates for the two sexes is in determining *which* turnover rates to examine. We know that for both sexes turnover rates are inversely correlated with age and that turnover rates vary by type of job. For example, if one is interested in deciding whether or not to place a secretary in a management training program, comparing the turnover rate of fifty-year-old male executives with that of twenty-five-year-old female secretaries is meaningless. The relevant question in that case is how does the turnover rate for a twenty-five-year-old female in an executive program compare with the turnover rate of a twenty-five-year-old male in the same program? And even after one has made that comparison, one still needs to ask whether any difference in those turnover rates might be due to differences in promotion opportunities or to institutional difficulties of the type Epstein has described.

The facts are that where age and type of job are held constant, male-female turnover rates are about the same.[9] It is, of course, true that reasons for turnover by the two sexes are frequently different. And employers sometimes feel that they have less control over the causes of female turnover. But the female turnover rate can be reduced by any company that conscientiously seeks to do so. Women who leave a company to pursue full-time child rearing do so because they perceive that the return for their unpaid work at home is greater than it is for their corporate services. Business can do a great deal to change the return parameters. Some businessmen feel that it is somehow immoral to try to retain the services of a woman with young children. It should be comforting to know, in this regard, that the large literature on the effects of maternal employment on children indicates that the children of working mothers fare no worse than others.[10] In fact recent articles discuss several *positive* benefits that children of working mothers may derive.[11] Paid maternity leave or sabbatical leave for several weeks, combined with the opportunity to work part-time for a while, may well provide the incentive a woman needs to stay at her job.

A second reason why a woman may quit her job is to follow her husband. But here again corporations can reduce family-related moves for women if they increase the opportunity cost to the women (and hence to their families) of leaving their jobs. Families who move to further the husband's career without considering the wife's job generally can do so if they feel the wife is not on a career ladder—precisely because the wife's opportunity cost is very small compared to that of the husband. Moreover, there are some women who, because of their spouses' occupations, are deeply rooted in a community. Physicians and lawyers in private practice and owners of small businesses rarely relocate, and in terms of long-range availability, their wives are often a good bet for managerial training.

We turn next to the second part of the problem: the failure to utilize women not presently in the business sector of the economy. Some women in the educational sector and women doing volunteer work have outstanding qualifications for corporate management. The failure to facilitate job transfer for women now in nonbusiness sectors leads us to overlook an important source of experienced managers. It also deprives business of different ideas, insights, and approaches to problems. Some examples may be helpful.

In December 1973 *Fortune* ran an article portraying several women executives in the volunteer sector. One woman, Marion Lloyd, chairs Chicago's Ravinia Festival. She helps to raise and administers an annual budget of $1.8 million. She directs 300 volunteers and 10 paid professionals. A second woman, Frances Loeb, is the New York City Commissioner to the United Nations. Without pay, Mrs. Loeb acts as New York City's liaison with the UN community of about 30,000 people. She supervises 80 volunteers and 17 paid professionals, and deals "with virtually every municipal agency as well as other public agencies and private organizations."[12] These women, and others like them, didn't start out as executives. They developed their expertise by working their way up. At any point in their careers these women could have been recruited into the business sector. The skills involved in running an arts festival are not unlike the skills involved in running a company. Within the business sector the practice of switching successful executives from industry to industry is not uncommon. For example, after thirty-five years with General Electric, Stanford Smith has become chief executive of the International Paper Company. Perhaps if business could consider the educational and volunteer sectors as "just another industry," corporations could begin to tap the vast female managerial talents that presently exist in those sectors.

A second major source of unutilized talent is the group of women who are seeking to return to work after having spent several years in full-time child rearing. Usually these women have considerable difficulty in "breaking into" management. In general they face the prejudice that given supposedly equal candidates it is far better to train a young man for a management career than to train a woman ten to fifteen years his senior. For of course, the argument goes, the young man will have a longer period of time in which to "pay back" his investment. This prejudice needs serious rethinking.

Two factors enter into the rate of return received by management from a training investment—the number of years the employee contributes his or her efforts to the corporation and the size of the contribution in each year. In making the decision to train an individual, the corporation faces a great deal of uncertainty. (1) Will the individual turn out to have the necessary managerial qualifications? (2) Will the individual be really outstanding? (3) Will the individual remain with the company after training? The key point is that the longer the track record of the applicant, the less uncertainty a decision maker faces. A decision maker has more information about the likely managerial qualifications of a thirty-five- or forty-year-old woman than he does about those of a twenty-five-year-old man. Moreover, the turnover rate for an older woman is likely to be lower than that for a young man. This reduction in uncertainty must be weighed against the fact that the younger man, *if* he stays, may render more years of service than the woman. And speaking of uncertainty, even the number of years available for rendering service is far from definite. There is the fact that women tend to live longer than men, although some men expect this advantage to disappear if women insist upon going into corporate management.

In any case, the point is that given the great uncertainty surrounding training decisions, it is by no means clear that training a twenty-five-year-old man is likely to yield any greater return than training a thirty-five-year-old woman.

4. Modification of Job Design

The final element in the short-run strategy is the modification of job design.

The basic reason for suggesting more flexibility in job design is that certain aspects of presently structured jobs cause the supply of potential female top managers to dwindle during women's child-rearing years. We cannot increase the representation of women in top management until we have significant numbers of women in middle and lower management. As career paths are presently fashioned, the ten or fifteen years between ages twenty-five and forty are crucial for potential top managers. Yet these are the years in which many women are involved in child rearing. As a result, they miss the opportunity to be "groomed" for top positions. When they return to the work force at age thirty-five or forty, they are presumed to have "missed the boat," so to speak. In the long run, it is possible that expectations about women's responsibilities for child rearing will be changed. But in the short run, the corporation has to deal with existing expectations.

Restructuring career paths may be accomplished, in part, by a willingness to train or retrain women who return to the labor force after several years of full-time child rearing. A second way to restructure career paths is by providing more part-time jobs at lower- and middle-management levels.

The part-time job route has some interesting facets. Top managers frequently ask, "What do you mean by part time?" The question itself is often indicative of the problem. Professional and managerial women with young children often have little difficulty in working forty hours per week. In fact, increasingly women with young children work full-time. Such a workload, especially if some of the work can be done in the evening, still leaves them a fair amount of time for family activities. But it is well known that young professionals and managers, especially those interested in promotion, spend more like sixty hours per week on a full-time job. And a sixty-hour workweek, of course, leaves very little time for one's family. Many professional women with children have said wryly, "I'd like a part-time job. I'd like to work about forty hours a week." And increasingly many men are saying the same thing. A recent article in *Innovation*, for example, talks about "mutiny" by executives (male) who are becoming interested in shorter workweeks and sabbatical leaves.[13] Not all women mean forty hours per week when they talk of part time. Some may mean thirty; others twenty. Some may mean shorter hours five days per week; some may mean eight hours three or four days per week. Generally, most are willing to schedule their time so as to make their jobs run as smoothly as possible.

From the firm's point of view, of course, not all jobs are

amenable to part-time hours, or to sharing. Clearly, for some jobs, decision-making responsibilities are such that they cannot be shared. But the surprising fact is that there have been few efforts to face up to the issue of deciding which jobs *are* amenable to part-time hours. And it is particularly surprising that so few have looked at the productivity impact of part-time work. Nor has there been much research on the question of communication among part-time workers or between these workers and others in the organization. The general assumption is that communication would be a problem. This assumption needs some study.

The fact is, of course, that virtually no manager is available full time for communication purposes. Meetings, travel, the entertaining of clients, and, yes, even golf may interfere with a subordinate or superior's attempt to "communicate" with a particular manager. Some aspects of communication may become more difficult when part-time managers exist, but the difficulties hardly seem insuperable. A female assistant vice president at the Federal Reserve Bank of Boston, who works half time, has recently written about the way she handles her job. Her remarks are enlightening:

> I am an assistant vice-president and economist at the Federal Reserve Bank of Boston. I am the head of the National Business Conditions Section at the Bank, and for two years I have been a part-time worker. My section includes one other Ph.D. economist, one junior economist, three research assistants and one secretary. My section has staff work with daily deadlines. We are often phoned by the President of the Bank to answer questions. How can a supervisor work part-time? The Director of Research certainly entertained some doubts when I told him that after my daughter was born I wanted to work only 20 hours a week. In large part, it has worked because while I am the official head of the section, I share my supervisory work with the other economist in it. Like team teaching, we have team management, with one member of the team being slightly more equal. I also have bright, well-motivated workers in my section who are happy to take responsibility for their work. I do about the same job I used to do, but for less pay. I also work harder while at the Bank. And of course, I take a lot of work home, which I also did when I worked full-time.[14]

Two final points need to be made on the issue of part-time work.

First, persons doing part-time work cannot be judged according to the volume standards used to evaluate full-time workers. By definition, part-time workers will usually accomplish less in toto than full-time workers, although they may accomplish more per hour. This point needs to be recalled when comparing part-time workers with their full-time colleagues.

Second, the opportunity to work part time should not be limited to women. As the number of two-earner families increases, more and more people—men and women—may be expected to seek part-time work. Some men may wish to work part time to facilitate a life-style that places emphasis on more than just work. Part-time possibilities allow the corporation to make use of *all* needed talent regardless of the number of hours per week the talent may be contributed.

Before leaving the matter of restructuring career paths, we need to discuss two knotty issues, the twin ogres, transfer and travel. Let us look at transfer first. Many corporate career ladders today involve a tremendous amount of geographic transfer. Corporations need to examine these transfer policies rather carefully to see whether current practices are indeed required. Frequent transfer places a great deal of stress on any executive's family, on a nonworking wife and on their children. As *Business Week* recently pointed out, increasingly, young executives, male as well as female, are balking at frequent transfer.[15] If the executive (male or female) also has a spouse trying to pursue a career, frequent transfer requirements can be devastating. Companies that do need to transfer people are going to need to come up with innovative solutions.

One interesting idea has been put forward by the State Department.[16] As part of its affirmative action program for women, the State Department has created family teams, where both the husband and wife are career Foreign Service employees and both are transferred together. In some cases, corporations may be able to adopt this idea. The possibilities for such teams are particularly good, of course, where a husband and wife share a job. But even where this is not the case, the possibilities for joint transfers should be seriously considered. A second solution to the transfer problem involves corporate cooperation. More and more corporations may find that part of the process of transferring a good man or a good woman will involve relocation assistance to the employee's spouse. This assistance can take several forms. A well-placed phone call may sometimes be of great help. Or monetary assistance may be useful. One company interested in transferring a woman to its West Coast office provided travel expenses plus room and board for two weeks for the woman's husband while he searched for a job in the Bay Area. The husband and wife are both in California now, both holding jobs they enjoy.

It should never be assumed that a married woman can't transfer. Even if efforts to find a new job for her spouse fail, the family may still decide that she should accept the transfer. Increasingly wives and husbands in dual-career families are opting to commute long distances or remain apart during the week so that one or both partners may take advantage of a particularly good job opportunity. (See Chapter VIII, vignettes by Thoma, Austin, and Levine.)

What about the travel ogre? Recently I received a copy of a letter from a woman who had just received a Ph.D. in economics and had applied for a job with a government agency:

> During an interview with a representative of the . . . personnel office, I was informed by the interviewer that "they" were worried about me, since they assumed that my career was secondary to my husband's and they did not want to spend money processing my application if all of my current and future employment decisions would be dependent on my husband's job. When I tried to explain that my husband and I both felt that my profession was the more specialized and that I would find a job first, and he would look for a job in that geographic area, the interviewer made the snide remark, "famous last words."
>
> Since the job of research economist consisted partly in becoming an expert on various economic problems all over the world, I thought it only reasonable that travel to those parts of the world would be included in the job. When I asked about the possibilities of travel, I was given an extensive lecture on how dangerous the world

was and how they could not allow a young woman with family responsibilities (a son and a husband) to travel away from home. When I asked if a young man with a wife and son would be allowed to travel, the interviewer answered, "We *don't* send young mothers to Uganda." Thus the interview ended.[17]

As Epstein has pointed out, employers who try to protect women often protect them right out of a job. Women *can* travel. Again the notion of woman as sex object may get in the way when companies try to see this issue clearly. When women are viewed as professionals rather than as sexual partners, fears about women traveling—alone or with other men—tend to disappear.

How much traveling any individual wishes to do, of course, involves a personal decision. But it may be particularly difficult for women with young children to travel. In these cases corporations need to examine the possibilities of cutting down on the amount of travel at particular career levels. Women may well be willing to trade travel time—doing less of it while children are young and agreeing to take on more of it a bit later in their careers. This kind of flexibility may be extremely important for some women.

B. STRATEGIES FOR DERIVATIVE BENEFITS

The benefits of the short-run policies we have been discussing are, for the most part, internal to a company. Although persons who transfer to other firms can take with them the benefits derived from encouragement, improved interpersonal skills, or part-time employment opportunities, by and large the companies that initiate affirmative action policies will be their own primary beneficiaries. Unlike the benefits of the short-run strategy, however, the benefits of the long-run strategy, for the most part, do not accrue mainly to a particular company. The long-run strategy consists of actions to be taken now that will yield benefits primarily in the future. As noted earlier, the long-run strategy is basically designed to bring about slower, more complex changes in people's attitudes toward women and their role in business and society. Society as a whole is the beneficiary of the long-run strategy, and the corporate sector stands to benefit directly and indirectly from more fully developing the potential of women as well as men.

1. Product Advertising

The first element in the long-run strategy is product advertising. Companies need to examine their advertising to see whether it encourages the aspirations of women and girls. The issues of product advertising and product demand and their relationship to women are extremely complex, but the demand for many products probably can be maintained without resorting to advertising that stereotypes women. In fact, among young people—men and women—sexist advertising may be yielding negative returns. In the near future, the National Advertising Review Board will be issuing guidelines on advertising with respect to women. These guidelines deserve careful attention. We need more pictures of women working atop telephone poles, more pictures of women managers, more pictures of women tinkering with auto engines. The images which women have of themselves are frequently influenced by the images portrayed in magazines and on television. Women are encouraged to become managers when they see media portrayals of women in nontraditional occupations and realize that these nontraditional pursuits are becoming acceptable. Women are also encouraged by television programs whose stories portray heroines in nontraditional jobs. One of the most effective types of affirmative action advertising might be for a company to sponsor a television program which stars a woman corporate executive.

There may even be immediate benefits as a result of abolishing sexist advertisements. Existing women managers (indeed all women employees) are encouraged regarding their own role in the company when they find that their employer's concern about motivating women includes the elimination of sexist advertising. Nor is the lesson lost on male employees. And if a company becomes known as a pioneer in fair advertising, it may develop an advantage in recruiting women.

2. Activities in Primary, Secondary, and Higher Education

Let us turn to the second element of the long-run strategy. Business can do a great deal in primary, secondary, and higher education to encourage potential women managers and to help young men to accept, and perhaps even support, management aspirations of women. Through pressure on school boards and through the funding of alternative materials, business can help to change the image of women portrayed in primary school books. As these books are now written, before children even learn to read they are encouraged to stereotype men and women. Many primers and preprimers present women only as mothers and not even as particularly interesting mothers. The mothers vacuum, mop, and occasionally rescue animals in trouble. Rarely do they read, pay the family's bills, or volunteer their services in the community. Never do they work—and certainly never as managers. Much needs to be done to open up the options that little girls see for themselves.

Corporations can also play an active role on the high school level. First, business can work with the professional organizations of career counselors. Career counselors' advice is often very important in young women's career choices. Yet as things stand now, high school career counselors rarely encourage women to go into management. Business needs to convey a new message to career counselors. It also needs to convey a new message to high school girls. Through movies and lectures, businessmen and especially businesswomen can help to encourage young women to go into management. Also, business might provide some highly publicized competition through which high school girls apply to work at corporate headquarters during the summer. Through such summer work and exposure to business, young girls will come to understand that management careers are indeed open to women. The message would be even clearer, of course, if these young girls could actually see women in positions of responsibility. On the college level, business can offer fellowships to women interested in pursuing management careers. It can also donate money to colleges for programs to encourage women headed for management.

In summary, corporations can do a great deal at all levels of education to convey the message that all talented people, women very much included, are being sought by business for managerial careers.

3. Child Care

The final component of the long-run strategy is child care. As more and more young mothers enter the labor force, it becomes increasingly difficult to solve the child-care problem by having each mother employ an individual to care solely for her children in her home. Alternative solutions for child care are required. Again, the issues are complicated and cannot be fully discussed here. But it is clearly in the interest of business to work with other groups in seeking creative solutions to the child-care dilemma. Not all solutions need involve full-time center care. Combinations of center and home care with special provision for sick child care may be far more acceptable to all concerned.

Some corporations may decide to set up their own child-care systems. But most companies will probably decide that the best course of action for them is to urge and support community-based child care. In any case, business should work for the *principle* of child care by funding research, by contributing suggestions and managerial talent to ongoing projects, and by working through the political process. A recent publication by The Women's Bureau[18] describes several innovative activities organized by particular companies to respond to child-care needs. These include an effort by twenty-five industries in the Benton Harbor–St. Joseph, Michigan, area to jointly establish a child-care center; a grant by a major corporation to the Day Care Council of Westchester, New York, to help expand existing day-care facilities; and special loan commitments made by financial institutions to both private and nonprofit groups for the construction and renovation of child-care facilities. Such activities by businesses encourage current women employees in their own aspirations. But far more important is the long-run payoff. As successful systems of child care are developed, more and more young women will be able to consider paid work as a permanent feature of their adult lives. These women will then be able to make more realistic capital investments in themselves. They will also require far less in the way of short-run affirmative action. All of this will, of course, be helpful to business.

Two affirmative action strategies have been proposed—one strategy designed to yield primarily short-run benefits and one designed to yield primarily long-run benefits. For the short run, we include the encouragement of women employees; the improvement among employees of interpersonal communication between the sexes; the modification of employee search procedures; and the modification of job design. For the long run, the reform of product advertising can encourage women to develop their aspirations, and business must be active in changing the sexist orientation of the educational system and in motivating the development of creative solutions to the child-care dilemma.

So far, for most companies, affirmative action has meant the setting of goals and timetables and the compiling of statistics within a personnel department. But affirmative action means much more. The problems it is designed to solve are vast and complex, requiring the time, commitment, and creative talents of the entire corporation—beginning at the top.

NOTES

For helpful comments on an earlier draft of this chapter, I wish to thank G. L. Bach, Carolyn Shaw Bell, Barbara R. Bergman, Francine E. Gordon, James E. Howell, Charles A. Myers, and Anne S. Miner.

1 Press release, University of California, Berkeley, Office of Public Information, Nov. 28, 1973.
2 See "Women In Management: What Needs to Be Done?" *Du Pont Context*, no. 1, 1974, p. 13.
3 Theodore Capwell, *The Sociology of Work*, Minneapolis: University of Minnesota Press, 1954, chap. 10.
4 See Michelle Z. Rosaldo, "Introduction," in Michelle Z. Rosaldo and Louise Lamphere (eds.), *Woman, Culture and Society,* Stanford, Calif.: Stanford, 1974.

5 G. W. Bowman, N. B. Worthy, and S. A. Greyser, "Are Women Executives People?" *Harvard Business Review*, July–August 1965, p. 164.

6 Ibid., p. 166.

7 University of Michigan, Institute for Social Research, "Survey of Working Conditions: Study Findings Challenge Stereotypes of Women," *Open Channel*, Oct. 4, 1972.

8 See U.S. Department of Labor, Office of Federal Contract Compliance, "Title 41—Public Contracts and Property Management, Chapter 60," *Federal Register*, vol. 36, no. 234, Dec. 4, 1971. The order covers nonconstruction contractors with the federal government and states, "Procedures without effort to make them work are meaningless."

9 See, for example, John B. Parrish, "Employment of Women Chemists in Industrial Laboratories," *Science*, Apr. 30, 1965.

10 Lois Meek Stolz, "Effects of Maternal Employment on Children: Evidence from Research," *Child Development*, vol. 31, 1960, pp. 749–782.

11 See Patricia Marks Greenfield, "What We Can Learn from Cultural Variation in Child Care," paper presented at the Annual Meeting of the American Association for the Advancement of Science, San Francisco, February 1974.

12 Eleanore Carruth, "Some Executives' Wives Are Executives Too," *Fortune*, December 1973.

13 Richard Beckhard, "Mutiny in the Executive Ranks," *Innovation*, May 1972.

14 Carol Greenwald, "An Opportunity for Business: Part-Time Employment of Educated Women," 1973. (Mimeographed.)

15 "The Case against Executive Mobility," *Business Week*, Oct. 20, 1972.

16 "Implementing Policy on Equal Opportunities for Women and Employment Abroad of Dependents of Employees," Department of State, Department Notice, Aug. 12, 1971.

17 B. Jennine Anderson, "Letter" to *Ms.*, July 1974, p. 6. Reprinted by permission of B. Jennine Anderson and of *Ms.*

18 *Day Care Facts*, Department of Labor, Employment Standards Administration, The Women's Bureau, 1973, pp. 13–15.

Chapter VI

"Perfectly Pure Peabody's": A Case of Affirmative Action for Women

The Peabody Soap Company was founded by Joshua Peabody, a small-town pharmacist who patented his formula for "Perfectly Pure Peabody's" soap in 1909. By 1973, Peabody Soap had grown from a one-product mail order house to a $100 million publicly held beauty business with 2,500 employees. The founder's grandson, George Hinton, now chairman and chief executive officer, had masterminded the recent growth, divisionalization, and international expansion of the company.

During the last ten years, Peabody Soap had received national recognition for its achievements in pollution control, community relations, and minority employment. George Hinton was personally responsible for spearheading activities in these areas, and he was proud of the company's fine record.

Hinton was known throughout the industry as a business

Reprinted from *Stanford Business Cases 1974* with the permission of the publishers, Stanford University/Graduate School of Business. © 1974 by the Board of Trustees of the Leland Stanford Junior University.

leader with outstanding instincts for developing both quality products and a sound management team. He began his career at Peabody Soap in 1945, having spent a year at a well-known consulting firm after graduation from Stanford Business School. He assumed the presidency in 1956 and became chairman in 1965.

However, in January 1973, the resignation of Chemical Research Manager Sarah Barrington (the company's top-ranking woman) made Hinton aware that he had not adequately addressed himself to a key corporate problem: women in management.

A. PEABODY'S MARKETING: 1965–1973

Prior to 1965, the company had limited production to a highly successful and profitable line of soap, shampoo, and related skin care products. "Perfectly Pure Peabody's" consistently maintained better than a 20 percent share of the face soap market. In the mid-60s George Hinton decided to expand product lines domestically and open up new foreign markets.

To meet the domestic objective, he promoted Herbert Richardson, a forty-six-year-old production manager, to vice president of marketing. Richardson, who had come up through the ranks, was considered a rugged individualist. His energy, directness, and work record made him a prime candidate to succeed George Hinton, who had already announced that the next chief executive officer wouldn't be a "member of the family."

Richardson's first move was to create a market research department. After a year of thorough market analysis by the new department, Richardson recommended that Peabody expand into the hypoallergenic skin care products field. Because the company had experienced little need for research before the decision to broaden the line, its chemical laboratory was inadequately staffed for experimentation. As a result of his industry review, Richardson knew that several companies were experimenting with hypoallergenics. He was convinced that the growth objective of the company depended on the caliber of the chemical research section and the speed with which it could develop new products.

A "blind" ad for a product research manager, placed in several trade publications, *The Wall Street Journal*, and *The New York Times*, brought in nearly eighty applications.

Richardson, who prided himself on his young and eager management team, was particularly impressed with one applicant—thirty-two-year-old Sarah Barrington, an unmarried research chemist. Barrington had spent the last three years as assistant laboratory director for Peabody's nearest competitor. Born and educated in England, she held a graduate degree in business economics and a doctorate in organic chemistry. Her total work experience was only four years, but she had an outstanding record with both of her previous employers. Furthermore, her salary requirements were low ($15,000 per year) compared with other applicants.

After her initial interview with Richardson, Barrington was sent to the company's industrial psychologist, who summarized his findings: "Sarah has good management potential, she is highly results-oriented with the proper balance of deference to authority. If, however, she cannot see the logic of a superior's request, she will seek an honest explanation. She is respectful, but also inquisitive and direct. She is ambitious as well, and will benefit from working toward long-term career goals." (See Exhibit 1.)

On the basis of her work record, the psychologist's assessment, and the knowledge that Hinton would be pleased to finally have a woman on his management team, Richardson selected Barrington for the job. In January 1967, she was named manager of chemical research and given full responsibility for setting up and staffing the lab.

Since fire laws prohibited the establishment of a laboratory in Peabody's headquarters, the research facility was located in a loft in a warehouse several blocks away. By March 1967, the laboratory was operational and Barrington hired a senior researcher, five assistant researchers, and a secretary. A year later, after a crash program involving close collaboration among the researchers, Peabody Soap was able to patent a process for the manufacture of "Peabody's Super Sensitives," a line of hypoallergenic products matched product by product to the regular Peabody line.

The sales increase of 50 percent over the next two years was

Exhibit 1　Industrial Psychologist's Report on Sarah Barrington: 1/5/67

Miss Barrington is a conscientious, industrious, dependable woman who takes herself and her responsibilities seriously. She enjoys her work, is ambitious for career progress, and is willing to work as hard as necessary to achieve her goals.

She is alert, intelligent, and perceptive of what goes on around her, and is eager to learn all she can about the processes with which she works. Her strong points are troubleshooting and problem solving; she is analytical, critical, and objective in her approach to situations of a technical nature. She works at a brisk pace, with strong focus on tasks, and takes pressure well. She plans effectively, is well organized and methodical, and can be counted on to meet requirements. She sets high standards for herself and others and faces up to issues squarely.

She likes activities that are challenging, stimulating, and rewarding, in which her capabilities will be utilized fully and which will provide opportunities for further growth. Initiative is readily available; she welcomes responsibilities and is eager to show what she can do on her own. She likes to explore wherever clues lead, will innovate and improvise as warranted, and is not reluctant to take calculated risks to test the validity of her ideas.

Verbal and social skills are very good. She is articulate, precise, and fluent or terse as necessary, and typically puts people at ease. While initially reserved with others, there is a warmth and dignity about her to which people respond favorably. She enjoys working with and through people and usually gets along with them. Occasionally, nevertheless, some people may be disconcerted by her somewhat unfeminine tendency to be forthright and outspoken when provoked.

On the job she prefers to set her own pace and be in control over her domain. Direction and criticism are used constructively, but she dislikes close supervision after assignments are outlined for her. She is most effective when allowed to participate in planning and decision making affecting her activities, given adequate authority for implementing them, and support when needed. Generally, she makes every effort to figure things out for herself before presenting suggestions or plans for discussion and approval.

Attitudes toward authority are favorable. She is appropriately deferent, cooperates fully, and complies and conforms as required to promote the organization's objectives. However, when directives or procedures don't make sense to her, she will raise questions and offer her views—tactfully but unequivocally. She needs superiors who are competent, strong, worthy of her esteem, and who keep communication lines open. Above all, she needs to be dealt with honestly and fairly, and be given adequate recognition for whatever she contributes to the overall effort.

Her outstanding trait, perhaps, is her impelling drive for personal achievement and career progress. And her strongest asset is indicated potential for further growth. Thus, while she is young and her experience is not extensive, and the fact that she's a woman will make her sometimes less effective, she should be capable of getting the new unit started.

due, in great measure, to the introduction of the new products. In January 1970, the company went public to raise much-needed capital for future growth—with funds earmarked for expansion in international markets. No new domestic product research of any magnitude would be required to meet these objectives.

Soon after the development and patenting of the "Super Sensitives" process the research staff was cut in half with the remaining members moving into quality control and analysis of new raw materials. Barrington received a citation from the board of directors and won an industry award for her work—but the company was no longer interested in expanding product lines. Realizing that she was at a dead end in her present position, Barrington hired a management trainee in 1970, so that she could prepare someone to assume her position. A year later the trainee was offered a promotion to assistant manager of market research. (Since he would receive more pay in the new position, company policy prohibited Barrington from refusing to let him make the move.) The following year, a similar promotion was accepted by his replacement.

In June 1972, separate product divisions were established. The work of the marketing function was to be phased out to the divisions over the next two years. At the same time, Richardson was promoted to president. John Carlisle, a distribution manager who was nearing retirement, was named marketing director. While most phases of the marketing divisionalization were easily achieved, the lab posed a real problem. Divisions were not interested in the additional overhead of separate labs. Yet they all insisted that a company lab was necessary. Carlisle had little knowledge of the lab function and did not care to supervise the section. To deal with the situation, he held a meeting of all division managers to determine to whom the lab should report. They decided on the quality control division and sent Barrington a memo informing her of the new reporting relationship.

B. EQUAL EMPLOYMENT OPPORTUNITY AT PEABODY SOAP

A family tradition of community involvement was a vital part of Peabody Soap's corporate policy. Joshua Peabody had a personal policy of donating one-quarter of his annual earnings to community organizations. His son-in-law, William Hinton, received nationwide recognition for his successful racial integration of the Peabody factory in the 1950s—long before such actions were required by law. It came as no surprise when, in 1967, George Hinton was appointed as one of six Presidential advisors on the blue ribbon committee "Minority Employment and the American Future."

Although laws requiring affirmative action for minorities were not promulgated until 1969, Hinton had set goals for the promotion and hiring of minority group members as early as 1966. By 1973, every Peabody plant had a work force which reflected the racial composition of its community.

Finding an effective equal employment opportunity (EEO) manager, however, had been a difficult task. After several men failed at the position, Richard Adams proved to have the necessary qualities for the job. Adams, thirty-five years old, had been a white activist in the civil rights movement in the early sixties. His understanding of the problem of minority employment, combined with his ability to establish good rapport with managers, led to his success in Peabody's personnel department.

Peabody's work force had always been about 50 percent female. While production jobs in some industries weren't considered "women's work," cosmetic soap manufacture was an acceptable industry for female workers. Peabody actually assessed potential plant sites based on labor surveys of the rate of female unemployment in the area. If the figure were high and other factors were favorable, the location was selected.

The precision involved in the work, clean working conditions, and low wages had also been cited as reasons why women were employed in the industry. Peabody Soap, like its competitors, had been slow in moving women into management. In 1972, Sarah Barrington was the highest-ranking woman in the company—and one of only four women in middle or upper management.

In 1971, federal legislation requiring additional affirmative action for women was in the wind. Hinton's own daughter was pressuring him to take a closer look at the underutilization of

Exhibit 2

To:	All Employees	December 5, 1971
From:	George Hinton	

At Peabody Soap, we have always been concerned with developing our resources—in terms of both people and products. It has also been our philosophy that discrimination, in any form, will not be tolerated here. We now recognize that women, as well as minorities, have suffered the effects of employment prejudice in the past.

We are, therefore, establishing a program of Affirmative Action for Women. Brenda Goldman, who joined the company as a secretary in 1968, will move up to become EEO Assistant for women reporting to our EEO Manager. Her responsibilities, aside from the implementation of the women's program, will include counseling, developing recruitment resources, and providing other supportive services.

In the year ahead we will intensify our efforts in the identification of promotable women.

At Peabody Soap EEO is a corporatewide policy. Every division, department, and facility is charged with the responsibility of setting goals and every manager is evaluated on the action he or she takes to ensure that our commitment is met. Monitoring the program, providing support services, and ensuring that all personnel practices are equitable are the duty of our Equal Employment Section.

It is my sincerest hope that we will continue to direct our energies toward EEO for women with the same vigor and enthusiasm with which we approach all other pressing business problems.

women and the related issues of day care and job restructuring. Hinton had an "open door" policy—any employee could come directly to him with a problem—and several women within the company had used it to point out areas for improvement.

As a result, Hinton asked the personnel department to add a woman to Adams' staff to handle female affirmative action. In fact, Hinton suggested his own secretary, twenty-seven-year-old Brenda Goldman, for the job. "She's been with us for five years now—she's bright, capable, and knows our management," Hinton explained to Adams, "and she's not one of those Women's Libbers. I hate to give her up, but I'd feel more comfortable with her in the job." Goldman became EEO assistant two weeks later. Announcement of her promotion included Hinton's policy statement regarding equal employment (Exhibit 2).

From the outset, rapport between Adams and Goldman was difficult.

Goldman: Where do I get started with the women's program, Dick? Guess I should begin by getting an idea of how we're going to be working together.

Adams: I'm looking forward to getting this women's thing started, Brenda. But frankly, we're going to have to hold back on anything big for awhile. Right now minorities—blacks in particular—are our biggest problem. That doesn't mean we're going to forget about women. You know, we've already made real headway. Sarah Barrington's doing a great job . . . she's one of the top 20 managers in the company. Besides, we're letting Carla O'Day and Helen Coates go on half-time jobs because they want to spend time at home with their young children. We've sent ten women to that "Women in Management Course" at company expense . . . we've liberalized our maternity leave policy.

Goldman: You're right, we have taken some excellent steps and most of the innovation came from you, Dick. . . . You must admit, though, that we still have monstrous problems. Look at the statistics. Women have a worse problem at Peabody's than do minorities.

Adams: I disagree. Black men have always had a tougher time finding work than have women.

Goldman: Dick, we could go around in circles about this. I don't agree with you. Black men and women both have had a tough time . . . and, I hasten to add, so do the other minorities—you forget about Chicanos, Asians, and American Indians. All of these groups are considered "Affected Classes" by the law.

Adams: Look, we've made progress and we'll keep making it . . . but we have to see this thing in perspective.

The conflicts were, of course, private; the reports which reached Hinton showed progress. To his knowledge, the EEO function was being handled well, and the company's reputation continued to be virtually untarnished.

Another aspect of the EEO operation of which Hinton was unaware was Goldman's image in the company. She had been accepted neither by her "constituency" nor by management.

C. BARRINGTON'S RESIGNATION

On January 15, 1973, George Hinton received this letter:

Dear Mr. Hinton:

It is with deep personal and professional regret that I must submit my resignation, effective February 1, 1973. While Peabody Soap has provided me with the opportunity to make an outstanding contribution in chemical research, I find no room for developing beyond this department.

The recent shift in reporting relationships in my section and the manner in which that shift was accomplished make it clear that my services to the organization are no longer of value. Furthermore, my ability to effect a promotion to other departments has been deliberately inhibited.

I suggest you personally audit your EEO Program for Women. Many problems with potential legal implications exist in the organization.

Thank you for your personal encouragement over the last five years.

Sincerely,
Sarah Barrington

Hinton, alarmed by the letter, called the personnel department and asked them to send up a copy of Barrington's latest review (Exhibit 3) immediately. After a quick reading of Barrington's review, Hinton confirmed his belief that Barrington was an above-average manager in all respects. Next, Hinton asked Richardson to come to his office.

The Hinton/Richardson conversation went as follows:

Hinton: Herb, did you know that Sarah Barrington resigned?

Richardson: No, George, but I did know she was unhappy here . . . it doesn't surprise me. For the last two years she's wanted to get out of the lab . . . but there's nowhere for her to go. She doesn't know any other function . . . and the fact that she's located in that other building just hasn't given her any exposure.

Hinton: Do you think it's because she's a woman?

Exhibit 3.

EMPLOYEE PERFORMANCE APPRAISAL

			REVIEW PERIOD	
			From (Mo/Yr) *December 1971*	*DECEMBER 1972*

Employee Name	Position Title	No. Months in Present Position	No. Months Supervised by Rater	Seniority Date	Field Location
SARAH BARRINGTON	MANAGER, PRODUCT RESEARCH	10	6	FEB. 5, 1967	ADJACENT LAB

Responsibilities Performed (To be Written by Employee)

List agreed upon objectives under each responsibility.

1. Complete tests for all possible new materials and processes '72-'73

2. Assist marketing group by notifying them of tests of all competitors' products

3. Supervise a staff of 4

4. Develop better exposure for lab to other functions

5. Maintain progress on X-22 project

Performance Appraisal (To be Written by Rater)

Evaluate employee's performance on each responsibility and related objectives

1. Excellent

2. Excellent

3. Sarah is a good supervisor

4. Sarah is progressing in this area

5. X-22 completed satisfactorily

OVERALL JOB PERFORMANCE

☐ Unsatisfactory ☐ Fair ☐ Competent ☐ Highly Competent ☒ Exceptional

COMMENTS:

ADVANCEMENT POTENTIAL

☐ Can Develop Further in Present Position ☐ Adequately Placed ☒ Ready for Advancement Now

COMMENTS

Rater's Signature	Date
John Carlisle	12/8/72
Employee Signature	Date
Sarah Barrington	12/5/72
Manager's Signature	Date
John Carling	

Exhibit 3 (continued).

Describe Two or More of Employee's Strongest Points:

1. Successfully delegates authority
2. Does an excellent job of training subordinates
3. Runs an efficient lab, needs little supervision
4. Very professional in her approach

List Two or More Areas That Could Profit From Improvement:

1. Sarah is sometimes aggressive... some of the managers she works with find this "puts them off." It may inhibit her job performance.

2. She could benefit from more involvement in management activities.

What Are This Employee's Career Goals?

For some time, Sarah has indicated interest in progressing to another management position. Nothing is available at present.

Suggested and Agreed Upon Actions to be Taken for Self Improvement and Achievement of Career Goals:

Sarah is our top female manager and therefore is a good candidate for promotion. To do so she must have closer communication with other managers. She would benefit from a little "softening" too -- being a bit more gentle in her approach.

CURRENT SALARY: Weekly   340

RECOMMENDED SALARY: Weekly   397   Eff. Date   Jan./1973

SALARY GRADE   20
CURRENT SALARY

    Min   Mid   Max

Richardson: Oh, George, I just don't think that's a problem with Sarah. She's had an excellent job and makes good money for a woman.

Hinton: How have her raises been?

Richardson: Well, since she's been in the same job all this time . . . and this wage freeze has been in effect. . . . Oh, she makes a little less than twenty grand.

Hinton: Well, where could she go?

Richardson: George, I don't know.

Hinton: Well, what about her reviews?

Richardson: They're great. She's good at what she does . . . we've been very pleased, as you know, with the contributions she's made in research.

Hinton: We've never really talked about her for a promotion, have we?

Richardson: George, I don't think anyone's ready for her to take over a major function as yet. We considered her for that International job . . . but, they just didn't think a woman could do the job.

Hinton: Herb, off the record, what do the guys think of her?

Richardson: That's a tough question. . . . Nobody really talks about her very much. . . . They respect her judgment . . . but we don't know much more about her. Her trouble is that she doesn't sell herself enough. She doesn't socialize. Frankly, George, I don't know what more we can do to keep her here.

Hinton: Thanks Herb, I appreciate your candor. Oh, one more question. . . . How do you think Brenda is doing in her new job? You're closer to the action around here than I am.

Richardson: To tell you the truth, George, I've been meaning to speak to you about Brenda. Although the figures are up slightly, I haven't heard anything about an affirmative action program for women, and from what I have seen and heard I think Brenda may be having problems. Just what the cause of the difficulty is, I'm not sure; it may be the setup in that office, or it may be Brenda herself. Let me do some more probing and I'll get back to you.

Hinton: You really think Brenda may be at fault?

Richardson: Well, it's possible. We just may have to move her out.

Hinton: Thanks, Herb. Let me know what you find out.

Hinton then called Barrington and asked her to come to his office. Traditionally brief at his meetings, Hinton decided to break the rule with Barrington to delve more deeply into her side of the story. The relationship between Barrington and Hinton had always been cordial and open.

Hinton: Sarah, I really don't want to accept your resignation. I'd like you to stay on. Tell me exactly why you've made this decision . . . and don't be afraid of chewing my ear.

Barrington: I joined the Peabody Soap Company in 1967 because, as I stated on my application, I wanted the opportunity to grow with a growth company. In fact, I chose to go into industry because I hoped to move from strict chemical research into other related areas of the organization. The reasonableness of that goal is evident when one looks at the experience of the two trainees I've had. Both men hold degrees similar to mine. I hired them at Herb's urging. . . . 'You can't get promoted until you have a replacement,' he kept stressing. Both Simon and Roger were offered promotions to other parts of the company. They make almost as much as I do now, and their work experiences and the exposure they're getting will make them more valuable to the company.

So much for what might sound like jealousy . . . and if it does, I'm sorry. I'm proud of Simon and Roger because I hired and trained them in the beginning. I mention them only as examples. In fact, my secretary was promoted to a training position in the Soap Division last month—so your affirmative action program does work.

But, back to my problems. Although I've indicated to both Herb and my new supervisor that I want to progress beyond my present job, nothing has happened. Other managers have been promoted from technical to nontechnical jobs. Take Frank Everett, he was quality control manager and now he runs the "Super Sensitive" Division.

My reviews have been good and have indicated that I'm ready, but when top jobs open up, no one even thinks of me. There was a job open for a research director in the International Division—it would have meant a big promotion in grade, pay, and status. I wasn't even considered, as I found out later, because they 'didn't think a woman could do the job.' It involved travel and dealing with raw materials suppliers—I do those things in my job now. And I had all the requirements, too. No one thinks I'm 'strong' enough to negotiate or wheel and deal.

When Herb left—I had thought that he was my real mentor—things got worse. Carlisle doesn't know me or what we do in the lab, and frankly, he doesn't care. I discussed my desire to be promoted and he simply said he'd get back to me on it; he hasn't.

You wonder why I haven't pursued it further? George, have you seen my last review? (He indicated that he'd just read it.) Well, look at the strengths and weaknesses section. Carlisle listed aggressiveness as a weakness. If I come on too strong, I'm considered 'brassy' or 'pushy' . . . and unfeminine. If I'm the least bit reticent, they think I don't have the stuff managers are made of. No one seems to be able to cope with the idea of a woman manager.

Frankly, George, I've been discriminated against for the last few years. I've never been promoted; I've never had much of a raise; I've never received a stock option; I've never been invited to the Annual Management Meeting . . . probably because it's held at the Downtown Club, where women aren't even allowed.

It's harder for people to level with me, too. Herb never gave me many pointers about improvement. I hardly got any feedback, negative or positive. The other men here won't treat me as an equal either and there aren't any other women even near my level in the organization . . . so I have no one to emulate or consult.

George, there really isn't anything you can do about these things, I know. I don't mean to sound melodramatic, but I'm honestly fed up with having to perform like I'm Superwoman . . . and being treated like someone's little sister.

Hinton: I'm glad you've been so frank with me, Sarah. Have you talked to anybody in Personnel about this?

Barrington: Yes, I did give Brenda a call and we had lunch.

We've known each other for a long time and I'd hoped she could give me some advice. She suggested talking it over with Herb. I did, but he didn't seem very concerned. . . . I think he's lost interest in me since his promotion.

George, Brenda's in an impossible situation. Adams hasn't given her any guidance in counseling; he's just made a statistician out of her. She cited two cases where she's afraid we're going to have sex discrimination suits—but she can't get anywhere with Adams. . . . He simply sees the women's program as a threat. Most of the women in the company don't even know who Brenda is. In fact, there's an independent women's group already holding meetings outside the company. It's common knowledge that Brenda is all but totally ineffectual.

At the close of their conversation, Hinton asked Barrington if she'd wait a few days before her final resignation. Barrington agreed and offered a handshake.

Hinton then began to consider his course of action.

Chapter VII

Bringing Women into Management: The Role of the Senior Executive

Francine E. Gordon

Once a company has become convinced of the desirability of bringing women into top-management positions, the next question is how best to realize this goal.

Let us start with an analogy. Suppose a company had purchased its first computer and EDP was about to be introduced; what would be done to facilitate this major change? Several answers are possible, each probably containing the same elements. A line executive would be appointed to oversee the conversion operation. This person would work closely with the systems analysts, the people with the technical expertise. Line managers in different departments might be involved in making decisions about changes that would affect them personally. Timetables and goals would be set by the executive, with each manager held accountable for meeting these objectives. Objectives would be defined in terms of performance, not attitudes. It is likely that such a major change in procedures would create tremendous anxieties among those affected, as well as some resistance to the change.

To minimize these fears, the company probably would provide some kind of emotional-intellectual support by establishing information seminars where people could ask about all the unknowns and could learn about the mechanics of EDP. The executive in charge, and probably the president of the company, would constantly monitor the progress of the EDP installation by making phone calls to or holding informal conferences with line managers and the EDP staff, or by requesting and reviewing progress reports. This visible concern and involvement by top management would reflect their awareness that the fate of the company might depend on the success of this conversion operation.

As the new EDP system was put into operation, managers would be evaluated against the objectives set for them to determine how well they had performed. Rewards and punishments would be distributed accordingly. For example, managers who met their objectives might get any of several rewards such as a raise or a bonus. Perhaps group rewards would be used, acknowledging cooperative efforts to meet objectives. Similarly, punishment would be dealt in a variety of ways—no raise, lower priority of promotion, transfer to a less crucial position.

The basic elements of such a program are (1) the appointment of someone with power to head the program; (2) the use of experts to provide necessary information and to consult on all aspects of the program; (3) the visible commitment of top management to success of the program; (4) the involvement of line management in the program; (5) the specification of objectives, giving direction to the activities of line managers and providing standards against which performance can be measured; (6) the focus of attention on change of behavior, not attitudes; (7) the provision of support systems to deal with attitudes and feelings; (8) the explicit evaluation of performance relevant to objectives of the program; and (9) the administration of rewards and punishments congruent with the evaluation.

Let us now examine the organization of most affirmative action programs for women. The situation at Peabody's, discussed in the previous chapter, is typical. The individual in charge of affirmative action for minorities is asked to include women in his (and it usually is a man) planning, or else someone, usually a woman, is assigned to him as the affirmative action officer for women. The qualifications on which the latter is chosen vary greatly; too often, it is assumed that any woman can handle affirmative action for women.

In the majority of organizations, the equal employment officer is identified with the personnel department, a department that has its own staff function, isolated from the routine work of the organization. With no formal authority of their own, the equal employment opportunity officer and staff are expected to design, implement, and monitor their programs. The involvement by top management often begins and ends with a statement, accompanying the announcement of the appointment of the affirmative action officer, expressing commitment by senior executives to increase the number of women at all levels of the organization. Unless there are also incentives for hiring or promoting women, most managers throughout the company begin and end their commitment to affirmative action by reading the statement issued by top management. All of this changes, of course, when the EEOC or OFCC does an EEO audit. Unless and until the company goes through such an audit, the affirmative action program usually lacks clout.

A. CHARACTERISTICS OF A SUCCESSFUL AFFIRMATIVE ACTION PROGRAM

Consider an alternative arrangement, a program resembling the one described above for introducing EDP. An effective affirmative action program for women should include all the same characteristics. Let us examine these nine elements as they relate to affirmative action.

1. Appointment of Someone with Power

There are many different sources of power: first, legitimate power, the authority derived from holding a powerful, prestigious position, best typified by the power of the company's top executives; second, reward power, the ability to reward or punish others (this power is usually coupled with legitimate power); third, expert power, the ability to influence others because one is perceived as possessing the necessary relevant information; and fourth, personal power, otherwise known as charisma.[1] However power may be measured, it is seen rarely among those who direct company affirmative action programs. If a particular EEO officer for women appears to be successful without formal power, the individual has probably developed sufficient expert and personal power to do so. If this does not occur, one way of ensuring that the person in charge of affirmative action has power is to appoint a line executive who already has legitimate and reward power in the company as the head of the program. It doesn't matter what kind of power the head of the program has, as long as he or she has sufficient power to move the organization and the people in it.

2. Utilization of Experts

Someone has to know what is going on. In the example cited above, the executive responsible for facilitating the introduction of EDP would work with the systems analysts because they would be the experts on computer capabilities. In the case of affirmative action, it is more difficult to define the necessary qualities. Clearly, whoever directs the program should have an awareness of the problems and a personal commitment to improving the situation. Beyond that, the expertise needed to accomplish the task includes competence in dealing with people at all levels in the organization, skill at responding to hostility and confrontation in constructive ways, knowledge of change processes in organizations, and an understanding of human behavior. If one person is proficient in all these talents, he or she may be able to develop sufficient expert and personal power to assume full leadership of the program. Should the necessary power be lacking, this individual should serve as the special advisor on affirmative action to an executive who does have power. The executive would be the official head of the program and the advisor would run it. Care should be taken to see that the executive selected is personally concerned with increasing the number of women at all levels—including management.

An important distinction must be made. The individuals responsible for affirmative action within the organization should be responsible for just that: in-house affirmative action. The function of affirmative action officers is to represent the interests of women in the company to management and to implement corrective action as needed. They should *not* be responsible for defending the company and its management against lawsuits, class action suits, or complaints from EEOC or OFCC. A separate individual or group of individuals skilled in affirmative action should assume the responsibility of representing the interests of the company to outside agencies. The two functions are discrete and not compatible. Affirmative action officers have been uncomfortable playing both roles at once.

3. Visible Commitment of Top Management

The attitude toward affirmative action on the part of the senior executives will determine the attitudes of the subordinates—at least those who are upwardly mobile. Good intentions are not enough, as Hinton found out. The commitment must be constantly visible. Peabody's organization chart does not reflect Hinton's commitment (Appendix II*a*). An alternate structure would be to move the affirmative action officers out of personnel and have them report to an executive (Appendix II*b*). Or if you want to leave the affirmative action expert in personnel, then a direct link must be established between that individual and the president of the company (Appendix II*c*). This could be thought of as a dotted line between the two on the organization chart, a line that really exists. Admittedly, this could be bothersome for the vice president of personnel, but that would be a small price to pay.

There are other ways to demonstrate the commitment of top management, as shown in the EDP example. The president and other executives should informally check up on progress by calling people, asking people to send up short memos on how well they're doing, inviting people up for a brief chat on the subject. To be certain women are getting equal opportunities for advancement, senior executives *must* keep a continuous watch over the situation. They can't afford to wait until trouble sets in before being involved. That was Hinton's mistake.

4. Involvement of Line Management

Involvement of line management, which should be included in planning and implementing all major changes, is often over-looked. Participation by managers, directly or through represent-atives, will facilitate change in several ways. First, it will ensure more accurate communication of information concerning the change and avoid the spread of panicky rumors. Second, it will provide information to the planners about concerns unique to each department or group. Third, allowing managers to share in some of the decision making enables them to experience a sense of personal commitment to the plans because they have in fact contributed in some way. This involvement could take several forms. The chief affirmative action officer could request line managers to form a standing committee on affirmative action that could assist in identifying problems, setting goals, planning changes, implementing plans, and monitoring results. To be efficient, such a committee would have to be small, i.e., no more than ten or eleven people. Alternatively, one manager in each department could serve as an EEO coordinator or representative for the department, working with the EEO officer on a one-to-one basis.

In all cases, participation by line managers should be volun-tary and provision should be made to free these people from line responsibilities long enough for them to execute their obliga-tions relating to affirmative action. It takes time to meet with the head of affirmative action, to record complaints of discrimination, to survey attitudes of male employees toward female employees, to develop strategies of change, to write progress reports. Failure to provide some relief from duties would undermine the program by making it more difficult for line people to carry out their affirmative action responsibilities and by demonstrating that equal employment opportunity was not important enough to warrant time off from the "real work." Affirmative action *is* real work, and it must be treated as such.

5. Specification of Affirmative Action Objectives

In terms of motivation, specific goals are more motivating than nonspecific ones. In other words, managers will work harder at hiring and promoting women if they are given numerical objectives that they are expected to meet. For example, a finance manager could be given the following goals: within two years, at least eight female market analysts should be hired, and within five years, 43 percent of all market analysts should be female. These are *not* quotas. The manager is not expected to hire *only* eight female analysts. The numbers are realistic guidelines of the number of *fully qualified* female market analysts the manager should be able to locate and recruit within the allotted period of time. These numbers are determined in part by the current and anticipated supply of properly trained women. Unlike quotas, failure to meet the objective does not necessarily mean the manager has failed. If this finance manager could show that all possible steps were taken to locate eight qualified female market analysts but only seven were found, and of these only five accepted jobs with this company, the others accepting jobs elsewhere, then the manager has fulfilled his or her obligation. The institution of goals also provides standards that can be used as bases for evaluation of performance on this dimension.

6. Focus of Attention on Changing of Behavior

It is generally assumed that since attitudes lead to behavior, to change behavior one must first change attitudes. Not so. The fact is that if behavior is altered, attitudes usually change accordingly.[2] If someone acts in one way despite other beliefs, and if that behavior is rewarded, lo and behold, the person begins to believe in what he or she is doing. Furthermore, unlike attitudes, behaviors can be readily observed, allowing progress (or lack of it) to be constantly monitored. Change strategies should focus on concrete variables such as wording of job descriptions, the assignment of jobs, and the treatment of women.

7. Provision of Support Systems

Change is often accompanied by fear. The introduction of EDP raises all kinds of questions: "Will I be able to adapt to the new system?" "Will I lose my autonomy?" "Will I lose my job?" Similarly, the introduction of women into high-level jobs is apt to create anxieties for men and women alike. Members of both sexes are uncomfortable with women in positions of power.

Subordinates are often resentful of women bosses; superiors are afraid to evaluate them and reluctant to provide them with feedback, particularly negative feedback; peers tend to ignore them rather than deal with the issue of how men and women can relate to each other as friends on an equal footing. Women in high-level positions may be concerned about their own behavior. Barrington, for example, in the Peabody case, was getting mixed messages as to how aggressive she should or shouldn't be. The presence of women executives may create conflict for other women in the organization, women who may have given up careers for marriage at a time when that was the norm. The latter may suffer emotional pain, and their internal conflict sometimes manifests itself in hostility toward other women in higher-level positions.

Many different kinds of support systems are available to help employees overcome these problems. Voluntary meetings of employees may be held to talk about the impact of having women executives. Small groups could be established where men—and women—could examine their attitudes toward women through role play, case analyses, and other assorted exercises. Perhaps a series of lectures could be set up, bringing in people from other companies going through the same change or from companies that have made the change. The possibilities are almost endless. In deciding which alternatives are best for each organization, you may want to consult with a specialist on the problems of bringing women into management. Names of possible consultants can be obtained by requesting the list of trainers specializing in women's issues from National Training Laboratories or requesting the list of consultants and trainers from Women in Action.[3]

8. Explicit Evaluation of Performance

In order to stress the importance of affirmative action for women as a priority issue, performance in this dimension must be measured. The most obvious measure is the degree of success each manager has had in meeting the assigned objectives. Other measures could include the number of valid complaints of discrimination registered against the manager by women or the number of valid commendations recorded by women for his (or her) special assistance in helping them with their careers. EEO performance should be included in the regular performance evaluation, and it ought to be part of the management appraisal. It must be clear that results are seen by top management and that the results are acted upon, which brings us to our last point.

9. Administration of Rewards and Punishment

While it is nice to be complimented for hiring and promoting more women within one's division, it is far more rewarding to receive a financial bonus. Actions speak louder than words—and until now, one of the problems with affirmative action programs has been that those in charge have had their hands tied. The system ought to work both ways. That is to say, good performance should be rewarded and poor performance should be punished. Willful failure to comply with EEO objectives should be reflected in decreased salary or promotion opportunity, just as exceeding objectives should be reflected in increased salary and promotion opportunity or bonuses. Reinforcement is a powerful tool when it comes to shaping behavior.

These are the nine characteristics that will ensure a successful affirmative action program for women. Decisions as to exactly how these should be implemented in each particular company will dictate the status of women in that company.

B. BASIC QUESTIONS FOR TOP MANAGEMENT TO ASK

There are some basic questions that top management or the EEO director ought to ask. These include:

1. Where Do Company Recruiters Go to Locate New Managers?

Every leading business school in this country is trying to find and to train more women M.B.A. students. Special advance notices could be sent to these women, informing them of pending visits by a company's recruiters and expressing the company's commitment to providing career opportunities for qualified women. It would be helpful to have a female recruiter on interview trips.

Female recruiters at some major business schools have significantly increased the number of applications by women, as an example. Other avenues are available, such as announcements in magazines like *Spokeswoman* or *Executive Woman*, which have readerships of professional women. Local organizations of professional women should be notified of job openings. A list of such organizations can be obtained from the Association of American Colleges. These rich sources are rarely tapped, and any company could benefit by availing itself of their services. All managers should be informed of these resources because so many higher-level positions are processed by managers and not by personnel. All executives have informal contacts in a variety of other organizations that would enable them to find out who and where the talented women are and then to go after them. It always helps when the initial contact comes from the would-be employer.

2. What Kinds of Questions Are Asked in Interviews?

Many recruiters are still asking women about their plans regarding marriage and family. Questions like these simply turn women off. Furthermore, if they are asked of women only, they are illegal. Measures should be taken to ensure that recruiters are not being unfair to women applicants.

3. How Are Job Descriptions Written?

As Meacham has explained (see Chapter IV), the issue of job descriptions has become a major one. Recent court decisons indicate that the law is becoming stricter about what is accepted as a bona fide occupational qualification. So that job descriptions do not raise problems—legal or operational—a corporation must be prepared to invest in the staff and time needed to review and rewrite all descriptions.

4. Where Are Women Placed in the Organization When Hired?

As Professor Epstein noted (in Chapter I), women are frequently found in noncrucial, nonvisible jobs, often staff positions. The career path of the personnel or the R&D laboratory manager is less clear than that of the marketing manager. Women managers must not all be sidetracked into staff positions.

5. What Opportunities Are Provided for the Advancement of Women?

Women need and want as much assistance in planning their long-term career paths as do men. They also need access to the necessary training—be it formal schooling, such as enrollment in an executive training program, or informal, such as movement through certain jobs for purposes of grooming and familiarizing the individual with company operations. One major subissue here is whether women are given a fair chance at landing top jobs. When jobs open up, women should not be excluded from consideration because of assumptions regarding what women can't, won't, or shouldn't do. The example cited by Professor Strober (Chapter V), keeping women out of jobs requiring a lot of travel, is a good one. The questions raised seem to be whether a woman could travel at all (since women presumably can't travel light), whether she'd be willing to leave her family for long periods of time (although it's assumed men and their families don't mind), and whether she should be allowed to travel alone (which has become a major moral issue). It is also argued that clients may be unwilling to accept a woman as a valid representative of the company, but the fact is, faced with a competent woman, few clients can deny her right to act on behalf of her company.

6. Are Personnel Benefits Fair to Women?

As Meacham has shown, the law requires that women be given the same insurance coverage, pensions, stock options, leave policies, and all other benefits as those given to male employees. In order to attract more women managers and to keep them, a company must provide extra benefits such as paid maternity/paternity leave or free day-care facilities. Such benefits are apt to be more important to women than to men for the time being.

It is hoped that top management, as well as whoever is in charge of affirmative action, will also want statistics on the proportion of women in management, the number of years it takes a woman to get any given promotion compared to the number of years it takes a man, which jobs are held exclusively by women and which exclusively by men, etc. Once these questions can be answered, top executives may consider several additional questions:

7. Are There Any Women on the Board of Directors?

If not (or even if there is one), consider recommending a woman for the next board appointment. There are women who are qualified to hold such positions, but they are often overlooked. Such an appointment should give added credence to claims of being an equal opportunity employer while providing upwardly mobile women managers with a role model, a woman in a position of authority.

8. How Many Women Have Served on Important Committees?

This count is not to include the women who have been on committees on minority affairs. The next time a task force is appointed, check to see if there are any women who belong there. This should demonstrate acceptance of women as competent managers and executives. It may also foster better peer relations for the women as the men with them on the committee are forced to see their competence—and are encouraged to interact with them.

9. If the Company Utilizes the Protégé System, Has a Woman Ever Been Sponsored?

If she is truly qualified, a woman's intelligence, skills, and motivation will eventually become apparent, regardless of initial doubts and reservations.

10. Are Women Given the Opportunity for Special Executive Training?

Very few women have been included in programs like the Sloan Program or the Stanford Executive Program; yet these programs are an excellent way of providing the necessary management skills for women who have proven themselves in staff positions—women like Barrington, in the Peabody case—and for women who have not had the opportunity to learn the ropes informally because of the male orientation of the upper echelons.

These several levels of questions and answers, actions and reactions, show how much there is to be done if women are to have a fair chance at making it to the top. The case of "Perfectly Pure Peabody's" is not inevitable. It is up to the senior management to lead the way, to plan and implement changes in attitudes and behavior, and perhaps thereby to change the world.

NOTES

For comments on earlier drafts of the paper, the author wishes to thank G. L. Bach, David L. Bradford, Anne S. Miner, Robert W. Simon, Myra H. Strober, and Eugene J. Webb.

1 John R. P. French and Bertram Raven, "The Bases of Social Power," in D. Cartwright and A. Zander (eds.), *Group Dynamics*, 3d ed., New York: Harper & Row, 1968.

2 Leon Festinger, *A Theory of Cognitive Dissonance*, Evanston, Ill.: Row, Peterson, 1957.

3 Addresses of all organizations and companies referred to in the paper, plus the names and addresses of other resource and consulting organizations, appear in Appendix I.

Appendix I

Consulting Aids*

Names of Consultants

National Training Laboratories Institute
1815 North Fort Myer Drive
Arlington, Virginia 22212
(Request list of trainers specializing
in women's issues.)

Women In Action
Helene Markoff, Director
Federal Women's Program
U.S. Civil Service Commission
1900 E Street, N.W., Room 7530
Washington, D.C. 20415
(202) 655-4000
(Request latest list of consultants.)

Recruiting Aids*

Lists of Professional Women's Organizations

American Association of University Women
Dr. Ruth M. Oltman
2401 Virginia Ave., N.W.
Washington, D.C. 20037
(202) 785-7700
(Request list of women's caucuses and
committees.)

Association of American Colleges
1818 R Street, N.W.
Washington, D.C. 20009
(Request recruiting aids 1 & 2.)
(202) 387-3760

National Referral Services

American Association of University Women
2401 Virginia Ave., N.W.
Washington, D.C. 20037
(202) 785-7750
(Compiles lists of professional
registries in major fields.)

*These suggestions are not intended as endorsement of the organizations named. Furthermore, the list
of sources listed beneath each subtitle is not necessarily exhaustive.

National Referral Services (continued)

National Federation of Business and
Professional Women's Clubs Talent Bank
2012 Massachusetts Avenue, N.W.
Washington, D.C. 20036
(202) 293-1100
(Maintains file of professional
women's résumés.)

Talent Search Skills Bank
Office of Voluntary Programs, EEOC
1800 G Street, N.W.
Washington, D.C. 20506
(202) 343-6286
(Maintains file of professional
female applicants.)

Journals for Professional Women

The Executive Woman
747 Third Avenue
New York, N.Y. 10017
(212) 688-4601

The Spokeswoman
Joanne Martin, Advertising Manager
1380 Riverside Drive
New York, N.Y. 10033
(212) 568-5007

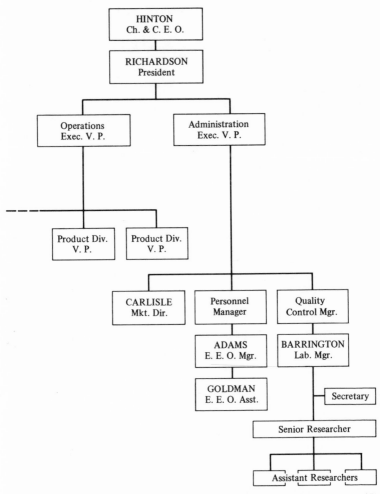

Appendix II*a* Peabody Soap Company organization chart, January 15, 1973.

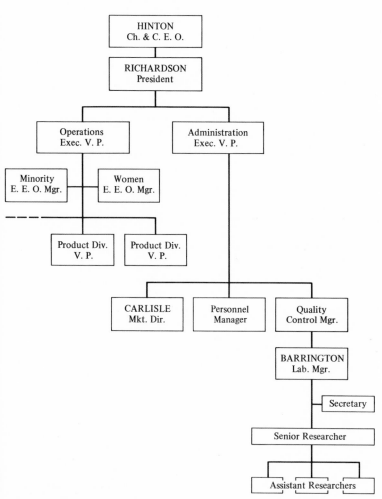

Appendix II*b*. Peabody Soap Company: a proposed alternative.

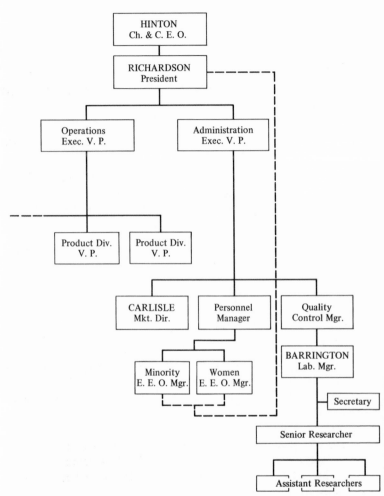

Appendix II c. Peabody Soap Company: a proposed alternative.

Chapter VIII

Women into Management: Vignettes

The following are real-life accounts of the experiences and concerns of several women in management: M.B.A. students, women who have entered management by traditional routes, and women who have entered the executive suite through less traditional avenues.

The discussions by Blanchette, Insel, Thoma, and Austin were presented at the Stanford Women in Management Conference. Those by Levine, Davey, and Miller have been written especially for this volume.

ELEANOR A. V. BLANCHETTE

M.B.A. student, Stanford Graduate School of Business

I'd like to tell you a little about my attempt to reenter the business world after some years that I took off to raise my family. I studied at the University of Birmingham in England in the early 1950s and majored in public administration. The early fifties were very exciting years in the health care program in England. They were the early years of the National Health Service, and I made a study of that service. After graduation, I worked in industry and for the Board of Trade in England, and then I taught the administration of the social services in a college in England for one year. After that my first child was born. Shortly afterwards my husband and I moved to Montreal, where I joined a seminar group of graduate social scientists involved in health-related fields.

In addition to my professional interest in the health field, I was rapidly becoming an expert in international obstetrics. My first child was born in England; my second child was born in Canada; my third, fourth, and fifth were born in Arizona; and my sixth was born in California. All this time I continued to pursue some part-time studying and teaching, and I always assumed that some day I would return to a career of my own. Meanwhile I was active in various voluntary organizations associated with obstetrics and child rearing. I found the years flying by very quickly with a group of small children, and then I found myself with the traumatic birthday approaching. I realized that thinking in terms of a future career really had gone on long enough and that if I didn't do something about it soon I would have to change my thinking and start thinking about where I was going to collect my social security check. Somehow if that happened, I would feel that the opportunity to really go out there and do something had passed me by.

Obviously there are enormous problems for any married woman with a large family who wants to be in a professional field. I am lucky in that I am able to solve those, but I would just like to mention in passing the sort of costs this means to me in practical terms. I'm doing a full-time business program at Stanford. I felt that if I were going to have anything great to offer in a new career I should go back to school and retool, so I have a full-time housekeeper. I provide her with a car because she now drives the children to the 2,000 things every week that small children have to be driven to in this society. And at the same time, we foot the bill for my Stanford fees. And I wonder just how many people are lucky enough to have the opportunity to do all that at my age. I think of myself as enormously fortunate. Obviously, my husband thinks it's a great idea also.

When my husband and I moved from Arizona, one of the reasons we chose to live in the Palo Alto area was the array of educational opportunities available. I had one enormous stroke of good fortune in that we bought the house next door to Jeffrey Smith, a Stanford professor emeritus of philosophy. Sustained by Professor Smith, who assured me that I had the necessary intellectual abilities and educational background, I called the Stanford Medical School and asked about their health administration programs. They told me that the business school at Stanford had a combined program with the medical school in health administration. So I applied to the business school. I had read that the business school liked to offer places to a very heterogeneous group of students, and I had the happy thought that if they had any little place marked for a forty-year-old mother of six, I would be admitted without too much trouble.

Here I am and I love being back in this world again, but at times I find my new life a little confusing. One minute I am a delinquent mother of six abandoning her small children for the harsh glamour of a career, and the next minute I'm a heroine of the women's lib movement leading my suffering sisters away from the diaper pail and forward to the executive desk. I'm not comfortable with either role. I had started a career in the health field many years ago. I feel that there are enormous opportunities in this field in the United States at a time when the whole structure of health care seems to be changing very rapidly. I very much want to go out and be a part of that. I think that business school here is a tremendous opportunity to work out the problems of integrating a family and a career. Obviously, there are problems. But I personally believe that my family is far better off with a mother who is happy here and now with her own role in life and with her career. I think that the time I spend with my children is richer and happier, though obviously briefer than it was before I returned to school. I also sleep a great deal less than I did before because it is after my younger children are in bed that I return to my studies. Neither the children nor the studies can have as much of my time as either one could if I were doing that alone. The frustrations of managing both in a twenty-four-hour day are sometimes great, but for me, personally, they are far outweighed by the richness of a life where I can study during the day and return home at night to my six children and my husband.

BARBARA INSEL

M.B.A. student, Stanford Graduate School of Business

I'd like to tell you something about what led me to business school and where I hope to go from here. I graduated from Barnard College in New York in 1966. Barnard is an independent women's college, a very independent women's college. I was quite sure that I could run the world any time I chose. At the time, I considered a career in investment banking. I had done some research in the field while I was in school. But much to my surprise, I found no one waiting breathlessly for me to knock on their door in 1966. I thought about getting an M.B.A., but in the early sixties Harvard was taking its very first class of women into its program, and the number of women in business schools all over the country was very small. Moreover, an M.B.A. wasn't a respectable thing for a young woman to obtain in 1966.

Many of my colleagues got law degrees and medical degrees; many more went to graduate school in the humanities and arts. I knew not one person who went to get a master's in business. So I went and got a master's in economics, and I spent the next 4 1/2 years as a consultant in Washington, primarily involved with the management and evaluation of government programs. Within two years I was directing major national projects and eventually obtained senior positions in the governor's office in Virginia and the mayor's office in Washington. The Washington public consulting business is a very strange and unstable one. When I left in June 1973, the turnover was about ten months; that included firms as well as employees.

In December of 1972 I began asking myself where I was going and whether I wanted to be doing in five or ten years what I was doing then. I decided I didn't. I wanted a career that offered me some stability and some potential for future growth. And I wanted to find out about that other strange world, the private sector or the corporate world about which I knew nothing. In order to do this I needed very specific, very different skills. I needed to learn about finance, accounting, and marketing. I'm the only person I know of who had to develop a cost accounting system, which I did in 1972–1973, without knowing a debit from a credit. It wasn't bad either. I also needed a time and a place to reevaluate where I was going, in an environment different from anything I'd ever been in. In this whole reevaluation process the only issue that was a women's issue was the credentials problem. It may be difficult for a man with a social science background to be taken seriously, but I found out from many people that it was nearly impossible for a woman.

In January 1973, I was in California on a business trip and I came up to Stanford. Two weeks later I applied, and a month later I found I was coming here. Why Stanford? Stanford had a public management program that at the time seemed to build on my experience. It had excellent programs in finance and management, which were what I was interested in. And I thought I wanted a career in the West. Now I'm getting what I want. I'm learning those specific skills that I sought, and I'm also getting exposure to a whole different world. I'm learning things like strategic planning and business policy which, I find, build very clearly on my experience, even though in a different sector. I find the experience exciting and worth the investment.

Where will I go from here? My main frustration with consulting was being in a staff or advisory role when I should have been in a line management position. Although I'm in the public management program, I will probably seek a career in the private sector. As I've learned more about that part of the world, I've become more interested in it. I expect to begin a career in some combination of finance and strategy. But beyond that I'm still learning.

I'd like to mention two issues that are very important to me. In those four years of working, I was often the very first woman in the organization, and even more often, the first woman to do what I did, particularly at the levels at which I operated. Being a pioneer woman is an exhausting task. I was hardly ever allowed to be tired. I was suspect when I was sick. I was generally expected to be perfect and was ready to defend myself at all times if I wasn't. And most difficult, I wasn't supposed to be emotional. For 4 1/2 years I wasn't supposed to be emotional. And we all get emotional. Some day in every firm there is going to be the first woman M.B.A. She may be someone I'm going to school with. I urge employers to be aware of the pressures she is under and to provide support for her in a very exhausting position so that she can do well.

Secondly, I don't really think that what I am talking about is just a women's issue. I think that perhaps the women seem to have defined it better because the movement has forced them to evaluate very explicitly where they are going. I hope the movement won't just be changing woman's role from housewife to working woman but will increase her freedom to create her own role. I expect that some day there will be no need for a women's movement. I'd like to think we're moving toward the point where we all will assume more control over our own lives, more responsiblity to shape our futures, to combine our careers and personal lives, and to make the inevitable demands on one another and society that go along with those changes.

MARILYNN THOMA

M.B.A. student, Stanford Graduate School of Business

I'd like to convey my perspective of the business world as a graduating M.B.A. and a member of a two-career family, who is just about to withdraw from the list of the unemployed. Having now completed several months interviewing across the United States, I have some sense of the degree of receptivity of large corporations to women as managers.

My undergraduate education was in home economics education, a field I chose because it allowed me to be creative and because the focus in all aspects of home economics is on that very interesting person—the American consumer. My intent for several years, that is, until I tested it against the realities of the job market, was to be a consumer service representative for a public utility company or to be a writer for a women's magazine. I had married and started my graduate study immediately after I received my bachelor's degree from Oklahoma State University in 1970. My husband had intended for some time to earn his M.B.A. and in 1971 entered the Stanford program. Our choice was based on the strength of the faculty at Stanford and on the teaching method, which seemed like a nice balance of the theoretical and the practical.

After we moved to the Bay Area, several things happened that encouraged me to look beyond home economics for a career. First in my student teaching and later in my graduate work in a field called family economics, I recognized and developed a personal aptitude for planning and organizing, an aptitude that some people might call management skills. Second, when I had completed my graduate work and I began to look for home economics positions, I learned that those positions were pretty scarce, and, more importantly, they commanded little credibility within the organization. So like many an engineer, I turned to business management as an alternative to the dead-end career that I saw as a specialist. I knew the M.B.A. program at Stanford would enable me to develop those management skills and tendencies that I saw in myself. The theme underlying this evolution from home economics to business I see as an interest in the consumer. That consumer is a very stimulating and challenging concept to me because it's a person whose changing life-style and social and economic characteristics have tremendous implications for the makers of consumer packaged goods. It is not surprising that the companies I was exploring for a full-time position included General Mills, Clorox, and Quaker Oats.

Now, it is fairly easy to manage one's own business career, but it becomes much more difficult when one is married, as in my case, to a person who is also pursuing a career. My husband, Carl, who is interested in finance and property development, received his M.B.A. at Stanford last June and has since worked in Phoenix, Arizona, a city that we chose because it offered him an opportune way to begin his career. Let me reassure you that we do plan to get back together this next year.* Early this year my husband and I tried a little of the decision science that we studied at Stanford.

*Ms. Thoma and her husband are now living and working in Chicago.

We each listed those cities where we felt our respective long-range job expectations could be met. After arranging our cities in order of individual preference, we put our lists together and identified those cities that were acceptable to both of us, namely, New York, Chicago, San Francisco–Oakland, and Los Angeles.

The coordination of two careers is proving difficult, but it has some very positive effects too. First, the decision process I just described makes it necessary to identify exactly what one wants to do with one's life and why. I would suggest that, second, a dual-career family is based or must be based on a high degree of respect, and it is also pretty obvious that the marriage is holding together because both parties want it to, not because it is the easy course to follow.

We are aware that our career interests and geographical preferences may change over time, but we agree that our respective jobs must meet certain minimum acceptable standards pertaining to responsibility, challenge, and salary. And once those standards are met, we hope to give each other as much flexibility and mobility as possible.

I would like to describe the ways in which EEOC applied to me as I interviewed for management positions. I found that the EEOC guidelines have provided some basic structural protection, but a great deal of natural curiosity and hesitation remain. Recognizing that curiosity about my mobility as a married woman is inevitable, I have answered such questions thoroughly but briefly, even though the EEOC would say that they are irrelevant. I am concerned that if I simply protest the questions, interviewers may make erroneous assumptions about the answers. I also typically ask questions in return of these corporations that will give me some insight into the interpersonal relations of the male and the female management in the company. I realize that being excluded from situations where those informal relationships that enable access to inside information, and being excluded from situations where the information is traded could reduce my ability to do my job well. And so I ask questions like, "Does Nancy go out to lunch with Harry and Bob?" "Does she go for drinks after work with Harry and Bob?" I also have a selfish reason for asking that, because I don't like to eat lunch alone.

A year ago I analyzed some information on the 102 women

who had graduated from the business school at Stanford between 1925 and 1970 to see what they had done with their business educations. Many had progressed far with careers as diverse as real estate, construction, and consulting, but a rather shocking 40 percent were full-time homemakers and mothers. Current trends in the United States, like the drastic decline in the birthrate and the tendency of women to join the labor force, have led me to expect a drastic reduction in that 40 percent, not only in my class but in the classes that have graduated recently. The values of my female classmates also convince me that an overwhelming proportion of female M.B.A.s are now opting for full-time careers instead of the traditional full-time or part-time homemaking function. I sense a very strong commitment among my classmates to uphold the image of businesswomen who can and will pull their own weight within the corporation.

MARIANNE AUSTIN

Accountant, Tax Department,
Arthur Andersen and Company

My entry into business school did not really follow a long and carefully thought-out decision process. It amazes me now to think back to my undergraduate days at Radcliffe in the 1960s. Not only did I never think about business school personally, but among my many friends who were considering graduate education, I did not know one who ever even mentioned considering business school. More than 70 percent of Radcliffe women do go on to graduate education, but not even 1 percent are currently considering business school. The major business schools deserve credit for taking a very strong initiative in encouraging women to apply, providing an answer to those who say that they can't hire women because there aren't any knocking on their door.

I thought most seriously about attending medical school, but after spending the year after graduation doing medical research, I decided that my interests lay elsewhere. I married, and my husband and I moved to Houston where he entered a Ph.D. program and I managed a small graphics gallery for Rice University. Thus I worked for two years after I graduated from college, but both jobs were traditionally held by women and entailed low pay and no real chance for advancement. I believe I earned less than $5000 a year, which wouldn't have even supported me for one year in college.

I had always viewed myself as one who would have a career, and when I gave up the medical school dream, it was something of a shock to me. But I was married, and as time passed I gradually, almost unconsciously, began to lessen my expectations of myself. The realities of the job market for a woman with a B.A. in biology were less than encouraging. I began to derive more pleasure vicariously from my husband's career than from thoughts of my own future career. If not for the series of fortuitous incidents that brought me to business school in the fall of 1971, I believe that I might have gone the route of so many well-educated and reasonably talented women, who could and should have had interesting careers of their own, but became discouraged somewhere along the line and transferred their hopes and aspirations to their husbands' careers.

During the summer after my first year at the business school, I went back East and worked for a large corporation whose top management locally was very committed to EEO and was actively seeking out women. My on-campus interview was the only one I have ever had in which my husband was never mentioned, despite the fact that I was being considered for a job 3,000 miles away. But my experience on the job was disconcerting. Top management may have been committed to EEO, but my middle-management associates did not seem to share that enthusiasm. Although my arrival was expected, no one greeted me on that first day. No one offered any work or any guidance. At lunchtime I was alone in an empty office wondering what time I should be back if I left. This benign neglect continued. I invariably had to take the initiative in terms of work, and even conversation. During the first few weeks I assumed that I must be doing something wrong. I had never felt such failure in my life. Of course, I had no peers or anyone whom I could really talk it over with, and I didn't want to be a boat rocker. By the end of the summer, however, I had talked with enough people in the company to realize that my being rejected was not related to my performance. I finally realized that while the commitment of top management may be necessary for EEO to succeed, that commitment by itself is not sufficient. The policy of equal opportunity for women must be communicated strongly and effectively to the middle management with whom women employees will be working most closely during the crucial early years of their career.

After receiving my M.B.A. from Stanford, I went to work for the tax department of Arthur Andersen and Company in San Francisco. I was a bit apprehensive about being the only woman professional among sixty men, but fortunately I had a totally different experience than I had at my previous job. I can say with certainty that I have in no way been discriminated against in this job either overtly or covertly.

I probably was watched a bit more closely at first, and maybe with more interest, than my male counterparts, but when I demonstrated that I could do quality work and that I was willing to put in long hours, which the busy season in tax requires, I think I came to be seen as an equal. In this field it is possible to make a fairly concrete evaluation of one's work, and this has been beneficial.

One potential problem that many of us will continue to face is that of managing dual careers. So far, when interesting short-term opportunities have arisen, my husband and I have gone our separate ways. The summer that I worked in New York City, he worked in Washington, D.C. Last summer he worked for a law firm in Los Angeles for part of the summer and I went to Europe—something that I had wanted to do for a long time and for which he just never seemed to have the time. Now that I am out of school, the juggling of our schedules becomes more complicated. My husband was offered the opportunity to clerk on the United States Supreme Court for Justice Douglas, an opportunity that he simply couldn't pass up. At first I thought that I would stay in San Francisco for that year since I liked my job. I was also reluctant to set a bad example, as the only woman, by leaving after only one year. But a year apart, 3,000 miles apart, might put strain on even the happiest of marriages, and I decided that I would really have to go with him. Furthermore, I thought it would be exciting. My firm was most accommodating, and the managing partner of the tax department offered to transfer me to the Washington office.

On the whole, business school has provided me with an entry

into a very exciting world and has changed my whole outlook on life. I believe now that my future is up to me and where I go from here is my own decision. I look forward to the time when I will be in a position to help give other women the opportunities that I have found.

DIANE D. LEVINE

Staff Vice President, Advertising and Promotion, Continental Airlines

This analysis of the development of my career and marriage partnership is a description, not a prescription. It reflects learning from my own experiences, a process that continues today. Each of us gains insight from our own experiences and those of others in differing degrees.

What I have learned from the past translates into what I currently do. As Staff Vice President for Advertising and Promotion at Continental Airlines, headquartered in Los Angeles, I am charged with building Continental's reputation for quality performance among potential passengers and users of cargo services. I direct a department of six whose functions include advertising, promotion, direct mail, collateral materials, and elements of marketing planning. This entails close interaction and coordination with the sales arm of the business. In addition, I direct four advertising agencies who generate our communications effort in forty-three destination cities spread across two-thirds of the continental United States, Hawaii, the South Pacific and Micronesia, and Japan. Approximately seventy-five agency personnel work on Continental Airlines and Hotel business. Our joint advertising and promotion activities are supported with a $15 million budget. It is my basic responsibility to see to it that this sizable investment is made in soundly conceived, effectively directed, and productively deployed advertising and promotion programming.

I have always believed, "If I am as good as I think I am, I can compete where competition is the toughest and rewards the most meaningful." This shaped several decisions: choosing a college; choosing New York City for a career start; and once established in New York, seeking out another difficult challenge in tightly competitive San Francisco.

When I was eight years old I began working my older brother's newspaper route. By thirteen I had enough baby-sitting money to buy my own clothes and determine my own wardrobe. By sixteen I had a part-time job in a department store to supplement baby-sitting. My quest for independence began early, was reinforced in my experiences, and was the basis for setting my sights on a career in business.

Graduating from Columbia Business School in 1963, I added an M.B.A. in marketing to the B.A. in mathematics I had secured at the University of Michigan. When I received the M.B.A., I had a number of personal objectives: (1) to control my destiny as much as possible; (2) to have a successful business career; (3) to have a successful marriage; (4) to enjoy a life-style that includes companionship, good food, and a stimulating living environment; (5) to prove myself in a man's world, competing where competition is toughest; and (6) to capitalize on my strengths.

During the almost ten years between my graduating from Columbia University Graduate School of Business and joining Continental Airlines, I advanced through four important career development positions. One was in an advertising agency, and three were in the marketing and sales functions of industry. Through the chain of career experiences, I have continued to learn and grow in four interrelated areas:

- Developing and refining personal objectives and values
- Dealing with "start-up" situations
- Balancing career decision flexibility with a fulfilling marriage
- Leveraging business experience for personal growth and increased responsibility

No one of these stands alone; all overlap, have required continued adjustment and fine tuning, and provide the framework for the remainder of this discussion.

While I was sure that I wanted a successful marriage, I had no idea what it would require. Since my husband, Matthew, and I fell in love with each other, two strong personalities have explored, queried, and challenged the changing requirements of our relationship. Within our first married year, I grew terribly unhappy with what I saw as the lack of imagination and excitement that had characterized our courtship. I blamed Matt entirely, and occasionally bemoaned aloud having made the marital commitment. We were forced to assess the trapped feeling each of us was experiencing. From this grew our very personal contract of "twenty-four-hour notice": our pact with one another was not for life, but for twenty-four hours, with renewal options daily on both sides—cancellation as well. This brought a spark to our relationship and the recognition that each of us is responsible for keeping it an exciting and growing one. The daily awareness of needing to work with one another to make our marriage successful has helped us over many shoals.

To date there have been six major moves that have helped further my career. Fortunately, my husband is my strongest supporter because he sees the growth and satisfaction one derives from a business career. As a result, he has made many accommodations to help make these moves, although some were accompanied by considerable risk to our relationship.

My first employer was the Xerox Corporation, in New York City. I initially demonstrated and sold Xerox office equipment, taught equipment fundamentals to salesmen, and did troubleshooting on problem installations. Within six months I was promoted; as a systems engineer, I helped develop additional applications of Xerox equipment in key accounts. Within another six months, I was offered a product manager position at Rochester headquarters, which, though an attractive opportunity, was not a geographic commitment my husband wished to make. We jointly decided to pass it up.

With my future at Xerox limited, I sought to develop my marketing skills, remaining New York–based, in a consumer packaged goods company. Lever Brothers was the choice. Here, under the guidance and direction of some of the most respected and demanding marketing executives in industry, I was put through the paces of learning the operating basics of advertising copy and media, consumer and trade promotion, pricing, packaging, marketing research, product development, and sales. During four years, I graduated to increasing responsibility on a sequence of product management assignments in the household and personal care (toiletries, dentrifrice) groups.

During my four years at Lever, Matt made a career decision to leave Citibank and join Scott Paper Company as a field salesman in Brooklyn. In one year he was promoted into the company's head office in Philadelphia. Since neither of us wished to give up our career opportunities, we "scribed arcs" from New York and Philadelphia, and the halfway point, Princeton, New Jersey, became the area for our residence. We commuted daily from the same station, Matt's train departing south to Philadelphia, mine north to New York City. Subsequently, I moved to American Home Products (AHP), also headquartered in New York, three times the size of Lever Brothers and a highly respected competitor in a broad range of drug, household, and food products categories. There, for 3 1/2 years, I assumed senior product management responsibility for seven toiletries lines generating $8 million in sales, directing five attendant advertising agencies as well. Matt at this point was back in New York City working at McKinsey and Company, a management consulting firm.

While we loved the New York City area, we realized, in the summer of 1971, that what we really wanted was California living—especially San Francisco. After much discussion, therefore, we decided to take the risk and move to San Francisco, although neither of us had any immediate prospects. Fortunately, after four weeks of searching for a job, I landed a position with Honig, Cooper and Harrington (HCH), a San Francisco–based advertising agency. There, as an account manager in new product development, I concentrated on two major accounts, a household product manufacturer and a food processor. In addition I authored a market development plan for a major West Coast bank seeking to strengthen its deposits position and contributed to the analysis and strategic planning in the agency's effort to secure the account of an international air carrier.

Thus in August 1971 we rooted in San Francisco—at least we partially rooted. Matt had sought a transfer with McKinsey, but circumstances continually postponed authorization of his move and left him no alternative but to resign. On payroll for three months thereafter, he launched Levine & Associates in October 1971, a highly successful venture headquartered in San Francisco that capitalized on his experience in industry and management consulting. Now he is president of Pacific Select Corporation and his clients include companies up and down the West Coast.

While I was at HCH, an executive recruiter called from New York seeking to interview me for a job with a West Coast–headquartered airline. Continental was looking for an advertising executive to manage its advertising and sales promotion program. The specs called for a person who had experience with consumer packaged goods, the airline industry, and account supervision at a large advertising agency. Ideally this person would be a woman. After interviewing with the company for three months, it was apparent to me that the opportunity was an exceptional one. However, it required working out of Los Angeles. And Matt preferred remaining headquartered in San Francisco, although he served clients in Los Angeles.

During the same period another opportunity surfaced with a director of marketing position for a San Francisco Bay Area food processor. I opted for the San Francisco job because of my concern about the effect on us of a 400-mile San Francisco–Los Angeles commute necessary in the Continental situation. Matt, on the other hand, believed the Continental position would provide the more enriching career growth opportunity, and persuaded me we should take the risk with the understanding that if it did not work out I could always return to San Francisco. So I set up housekeeping in Los Angeles. Within one month, we were delighted to discover that the new arrangement was enhancing our relationship. After eleven years of marriage, we were dating again. We now have homes in both cities. I am in San Francisco only 10 percent of the time, but Matt is in Los Angeles half the nights, and so we are never away from one another more than three nights each week. Furthermore, if I do get lonely, I catch a quick plane, as I frequently do midweek, and go to San Francisco for dinner with Matt. Living on the beach near the airport has made this a convenient option. Our life-style has become sharing on a 50-50 basis: contributions and rewards, household chores, cooking, shopping, and financial management.

So far, in each career move I have been the first woman to reach a particular level. This is what is meant by start-up situations. I was not intent on pioneering, but little else was available during the past ten years.

It is very difficult to be first. Uncomfortable working environments are not unusual. One is in a corporate fishbowl, and problems emerge from this exposure vis-à-vis other women in the organization who are for the most part quite negative. Other women tend to aspire to the same responsibilities without understanding what is required to obtain or earn them. Many are sympathetic and interested, but some evidence resentment and/or hypersensitivity. Personnel consultants suggest, and I agree, that if a company decides to hire an out-of-the-mold "foreigner," it is better for all concerned to hire at least two, not just one. It is extremely difficult for one individual to influence a corporate environment.

My peers have usually felt highly competitive with me and have felt threatened by my success. The exceptions are usually extremely capable people who welcome my "Let's get it done" attitude. Often, male peers feel I offer unfair competition and represent an easy "straw person" to attack. Being the only woman in management provides some with an easy target or an immediate issue to rally against.

On the other hand my superiors have become great supporters, interested in the results of the productivity they see in my efforts to prove myself and in my unwillingness to take things for granted. Similarly, subordinates find it rewarding to work with me insofar as the goals are clear-cut and well understood; I let them know that if they work hard and do a good job, they'll be rewarded.

As mentioned earlier, these experiences have provided a most varied and exciting life and life-style to date. I hope it will continue to be so.

MARY C. DAVEY

Director, Midpeninsula Citizens for Fair Housing

In June 1951 I married my Air Force husband and a year later graduated from Smith College with a B.A. degree in English. During my final Chaucer exam, our first child announced his vigorous existence by kicking throughout the last bluebook I was to fill. After a few months, prospects of job finding or graduate study in the Air Force slipped further and further away. Need I say the early fifties were immensely different from the seventies —and so were we! However, five years and three children later, civilianized, I was ready for something other than one-syllable words and vintage Spock.

I became a professional volunteer. The pay was poor, but the hours were flexible—a necessity with three small children. Since early high school, I had been interested in community service—a by-product of coming from the Midwestern upper-middle class and the inevitable Junior League associations. But I was intrigued by another league—the League of Women Voters (I am a twenty-year veteran of both leagues). And that was where my first serious volunteer experience began.

I started at the bottom, attending meetings and doing the scut work nobody else wanted to do. I was eventually recognized as dependable—even bright—and was given a project: water resources. I did research, read, interviewed experts, made trips, organized and led discussions. But most important, I learned about the community and how it functioned. Practically speaking, I learned more than I ever had in college. In the Baltimore County League I did what in essence turned out to be a dissertation on water resources in the mid-Atlantic states. It coped with the intricacies and obscurities of the Corps of Engineers and state and local governments, and their budgets and powers. The work carried a certain amount of responsibility, which I enjoyed, but also led to a certain amount of frustration because it was not always feasible to act on the information and the recommendations.

This fact finding, education, and analysis aimed at constructive action inevitably led me to politics, elective office, and the utilization of information to accomplish change. It also led me to perceive and pursue the two major themes of community service in my life—concern for environmental resources and an equal concern for human resources, or human rights.

With this activist zeal and interest, I was an easy mark in politics for any volunteer job. I organized every campaign in sight, directed large numbers of people for worthy causes, and raised lots of money. While money raising was anathema to many, particularly volunteers, it never bothered me because I liked to spend it on first-rate campaigns or give it to good causes. I figured if you liked to spend it, you'd better raise it.

One thing led to another, and after moving to California I served for seven years on a local city council, with two two-year stints as deputy mayor. On behalf of the town, I served on several regional governmental bodies as well during those years, and was involved in countywide and statewide committees on specific programs, among them the Involvement Corps, Economic Opportunity Program, the Aging, and Fair Housing. I was also active in partisan politics at the local, statewide, and national levels, including several congressional campaigns and one national convention. I wrote a newspaper column for a county weekly, and kept in constant contact with the media on behalf of various organizations in the areas of environmental concern and housing. I received awards for outstanding community service, was Ford Motor Company's "Citizen of the Year," and was included in a nationwide article in *This Week* magazine (May 4, 1969) entitled "Women Who Get Things Done."

I list all these laurels reluctantly, but I do so to indicate that when I burst upon an unsuspecting job market, it was hardly my first venture away from hearth and home. I had had twenty years of volunteer service, much of it in positions of pressure and responsibility. Now my husband had fled the corporate world to establish his own business and we needed a second income to survive. I had to find a job within four months.

With his help and some additional professional guidance, I prepared a zingy résumé and scattered it widely. My targets were selected public and private agencies along with a few businesses that sounded appealing. Positions sought fell roughly into management/administrative, community organization, public service, or community relations positions. Some examples (they will remain nameless, but I would love to tell on some of them) are:

- City of 100,000—administrative assistant in community service department
- Countywide private service agency—community organization director
- County government agency—assistant administrator, affirmative action programs
- Local business—assistant community relations director

Of the seventy-five résumé recipients, there was dead silence from about two-thirds. Upon telephone follow-up to those (I soon learned not to follow up by letter—more silence) I was usually given an exquisitely polite brush-off, or a "We'll be sure to file your résumé for future reference," or four patent variations of the runaround. I recognized them all, having used them myself once upon a time at the other end. Not one résumé sent out in response to a newspaper ad led anywhere.

Sixteen contacts eventually led to interviews. This was encouraging until I went to the first one. I arrived promptly, with three working pens to fill out more papers, and was eventually ushered into the director's office. Looking over my résumé she asked me if I was Mrs. Davey, and I said, "Yes," whereupon she looked accusingly at me and said, "I see that you have never worked before." I must have appeared somewhat startled, because before I could say "Yes, but . . . ," she announced that it was the policy of the agency "not to hire people who had never worked before." They had had some "bad experiences" with people like me and had made it a firm policy. I didn't even get to leave her the additional forms I had filled out. The "interview" had lasted all of four minutes.

On the way home I bought a flowering petunia to bolster my morale. I was sure this first interview was a fluke and the remaining fifteen would be better. They weren't, except they got longer. The added minutes were spent hearing statements to the effect that I had never drawn a steady paycheck; "But you have no experience, Mrs. Davey"; why was a resident of a well-to-do community out looking for work? "Didn't I realize there were others who *needed* employment?"; being "over forty with no advanced degrees" or "no managerial background really puts you out of the running, Mrs. Davey, but you really have done some wonderful things." My protests about equivalencies were futile. It made little difference that in my volunteer board or elective experience I had dealt with million-dollar budgets and hired and fired numerous employees.

About halfway through all this, with my husband and family cautiously eyeing me for some good news, I wondered what on earth I was doing wrong or what was wrong with everyone else. I questioned friends in positions similar to those I was seeking, and their advice was to continue on as advertised but to use what political influence or pull I had. I told myself I was not about to do that because I honestly believed my qualifications were sufficient to obtain responsible paid employment. My pride also stood in the way.

After the sixteenth interview, my self-confidence hanging limply around my ankles, I called a friend who was employed in a regional housing agency where I had heard there was soon to be an opening for director. The post had not yet been vacated or the position advertised. I asked her if the agency had interviewed anyone; she said no but they had someone in mind who had done some work for them. I said I was interested and she seemed pleased and promised to pass on the information to the president and board of directors. I knew most of them and they knew me. As a matter of fact, I had been one of the founders of the agency and had served on the board for several years.

That was the breakthrough. I was hired within two weeks and went to work on the day of my four-month deadline. As it turned out, my qualifications in public service were very important to this particular agency, but it was also an enormous plus that most of the board knew me. For the time being, it is very important for women in management to have pieces of paper that say they are qualified. Or friends in responsible positions.

Now that I have been director of this agency for 2 1/2 years, there is easy acceptance by associates and much less skepticism. It is as if I had proved myself and all those claims to be true. Skeptics have become believers in a few cases; the way may be a bit easier for the next. I have received other and better job offers. Perhaps I may pursue them now that the breakthrough has occurred.

Meanwhile, some personal observations:

1. For the most part, equivalencies in volunteer work experience aren't worth a damn in the paid world.

You can make all the claims in the world about having hired, directed, and fired professional staffs or volunteers, raised and spent thousands of dollars, and accomplished all sorts of things like running shops that gross huge amounts of money each year, but the personnel interviewer really doesn't believe you. Nothing could be done well if you are not being paid. You can even come out in the top 5 percent on the employment tests—statistics, management structure, buzz words, and all—but you just couldn't be as good as if you had been paid. If you were as good, in a sense that would put the lie to everything that employers had been doing for years.

It may also be that many people in management and personnel really do not know very much about the volunteer world except what they read in the papers, which is usually the glamorous fund raising social event that connotes frivolity and snobbery. How could anything like that possibly require management and organizational skills? Finally, it is very hard to convince someone that you like to work if, by his or her criteria, you have never done so.

2. Women interviewers are prone to be harder on the older female applicant wanting to enter the management field.

I kept trying to figure this one out, because I had thought it would really be the men who would give me a hard time. True, in a few cases I ran into the totally hopeless male chauvinist, but that was *not* the rule. Most men were rather sensitive, particularly if they had nothing to do with engineering or technology. I guess it was because I was beyond the sex object age and my children would no longer keep me home from work.

But the women. Why the veiled hostility? I finally concluded that they felt threatened or undermined by my wanting to enter management at a higher level than their points of entry. I—the newcomer—had not paid my dues as had been demanded of them over the years of steady paid employment. Why had I any right early on to expect something so long in coming to them?

3. Unpaid elective officeholding doesn't qualify you for anything except skepticism and sympathy.

The average person interviewing you for the job believes that all you do is to make ethereal policy decisions while the city staff runs the show. You can protest that you hire the staff, especially the city manager and the department heads, but the interviewer discounts that; you had to have a manager, didn't you?

One could talk endlessly about developing multimillion-dollar budgets, making decisions about what or what not to cut, instituting new services or programs, forming sewer assessment districts that affect many peoples' lives, but to little avail. For some reason that does not count; it is even a liability in some cases because of the inevitable political scuffles that involve running the most humble community.

One further footnote: the "someone in mind" who was slated to get the housing agency job that I snared entered graduate school in business. With her new M.B.A. she is now working in Washington, making 2 1/2 times my salary. Obviously that is the way to break into management.*

PAT MILLER

President, Family Planning Alternatives

Frequently women are told, "If you can't get a job, volunteer. At least you can get your foot in the door that way." I suppose I would have to say this worked for me; I have wondered occasionally what my career path might have been had I not served as a volunteer. Being a volunteer gave me the inspiration to look for a job. Unfortunately, though, employers were not inspired to hire me.

*Ms. Davey has recently become an administrator with Economic and Social Opportunities, Inc., earning twice her previous salary.

Depressing as the search was, I do not any longer blame those employers who missed their golden opportunity. At the time, I was convinced that my enormous talents should be obvious to anyone who would take the time to review my résumé. After having reviewed more than my share of job applications, however, I now realize that few employers have the interpretive skills that would have been required to ferret out my special talents.

Stated briefly, I married, obtained a B.S. degree from Purdue University in English literature, worked for nearly four years in the public library near that university, attended the University of Chicago for two quarters, worked a year and a half in the correspondence department at Standard Oil, became a mother, obtained an M.A. degree from Stanford University in anthropology, became a foster mother, did the required course work for a Ph.D., became a volunteer with Planned Parenthood, and looked for a job—in roughly that order. It had been interesting and fun, but for all of it, I arrived at the age of thirty-eight with little to excite a prospective employer.

There were some indications that I was not completely without ability. For instance, while making excellent grades at Purdue, I kept house and worked twenty to thirty hours a week at the library. Without unusual energy and organizational skills, this would have been an impossible feat. At the library, after starting in the lowest possible position, a page, I left as an assistant librarian with full charge of the children's department. Promotions had come quickly at Standard Oil as well. At Stanford, I managed a household for a busy and gregarious husband and cared for our own young son and a physically and emotionally handicapped foster son while carrying a full load of course work—showing, I think, that my energy had lessened not at all in the years since my undergraduate degree.

It was at Planned Parenthood, though, that I "found myself." At the urging of a friend, I accepted the responsibility for that organization's educational program—a task, I was told, that would take five to eight hours a week. I became fully involved at once. In this one field, I could further several of my interests: equalization of opportunities for women, the population problem, aiding of the poor, sex education for the young, etc. Within three months, I was working forty to sixty hours a week, still as a volunteer. But now I was serving on the executive committee of the board of directors, writing all the brochures used by the organization, doing most of the fund raising and all the public relations work, training the new volunteers, and designing a training program for pregnancy counselors. When the executive director resigned, I applied for the job.

Then the "fun" began. The interview with the personnel committee was disastrous! The chairman began by asking me how fast I typed, to which I replied that the question was not relevant. Half an hour later we were still on the same subject— my typing. I could type—about 70 words a minute—but my concept of the job did not include exercising this skill. When it became painfully evident that I would not discuss my typing skills or lack thereof, he went on to the next (and last) question: if hired, did I really think I could keep up with the demands of both job and family. With that I terminated the interview. Shortly thereafter, a man was hired and without a single question about his typing. I did not resent my failure to get the job. I did resent the quality of the interview.

Disastrous though the interview was, having once screwed up my courage to face it, I could no longer be content with working as a volunteer. I began to search seriously for something interesting to do for which someone was willing to pay. The next five months were devastating. I knew my degrees were practically worthless as job credentials and my "work" experience was not recent. Nevertheless, I did think that my record taken altogether would show I was capable of doing something. I will admit I had no idea myself what that something might be. I followed up every lead: newspaper ads, personnel agency notices, etc.

I was overeducated and underqualified. The job would bore me, or it required a particular degree I did not have. And I immediately learned that volunteer work, even when documented and described in glowing letters, counts for nothing. Only paid employment counts. Just when I was becoming terribly dis- couraged, Planned Parenthood fired the executive director and this time the board offered me the job.

The first few months were rough; after wanting the position, I felt totally inadequate to handle it. I had never hired or dismissed anyone and had to learn both quickly. I knew very little about bookkeeping or accounting. Budgeting for the organization proved to be more difficult than I had imagined. Nothing was easy, and I made more mistakes than I like to remember. I had to learn fast and help was not easy to find. Or so I thought.

Only recently have I come to realize the extent to which my feeling of inadequacy was created out of fear of failure more than actual deficiencies. No one finds hiring or firing easy. And budgets, when there is not much money to work with, can never be easy.

When I resigned from Planned Parenthood two years later, I was a different person—far more self-assured and much more "salable." That was three years ago, when with two others I began the formation and development of an organization designed to take up the family planning problem where Planned Parenthood stops. Our organization, Family Planning Alternatives, was set up with a loan of $4,000 to provide infertility diagnosis, birth control information, male and female sterilization, and abortion. It was begun as an experiment, an attempt to determine whether it was possible to provide these services at low cost, with highly qualified personnel compensated adequately, without having to solicit financial support. Our annual budget is now over $500,000, and the experiment has proved highly successful.

I am president of Family Planning Alternatives, with responsibilities that include budget preparation, public relations, liaison between the board and the staff, liaison to other groups involved in related areas, and personnel administration of major positions. The experience gained at Planned Parenthood has been invaluable in at least two ways: it showed the community that I was capable of handling an important managerial position, and, perhaps even more important, it demonstrated the same thing to me, a woman over forty, feeling the excitement of a new beginning.

Chapter IX

Conclusion: Problems and Opportunities

Myra H. Strober
Francine E. Gordon

There is an unmistakable, almost contagious, sense of excitement and expectation in the vignettes of the preceding chapter. Although the women portrayed have known difficulties and disappointments, nonetheless they exhibit a tremendous optimism and exhilaration. Even Davey, whose setbacks have been so many and so unjust, is ultimately optimistic "now that the breakthrough has occurred."

This sense of excitement is hardly surprising. It results from at least two factors. The first is personal. To state it simply, business careers can be tremendously stimulating. Men have always known this, but women, for the most part, have known it only indirectly, as observers. Much of this excitement stems from the opportunity to face challenges personally, with resulting rewards and punishments. Thus Blanchette writes of the new "richness of . . . life" she experiences in combining the mother-wife and student roles. Pat Miller notes the tremendous excitement of a new beginning for a woman over forty, and Levine stresses the diversity and reward of her life and life-style.

The second reason for the excitement is perhaps even more important, for it goes beyond individual satisfaction. It stems from anticipation of profound and widespread change. Thus Insel looks forward to a time when both women and men will assume more control over their lives. Austin discusses her potential to help other women, and Thoma, contrasting recent women M.B.A.s with those of the past, is gratified by the new strong career commitment she finds among her classmates.

With redefinitions of the role of women in business, as represented by the vignettes, we are just beginning to realize how much change is possible. But every readjustment has its costs. Disequilibrium brings with it uncomfortable uncertainties and contradictions. In concluding this volume we look at both aspects of the current disequilibrium, first reviewing problems and then discussing some new opportunities for business that may arise from bringing women into management.

A. REVIEW OF MAJOR PROBLEMS

Four major barriers hinder the entry of women into management: (1) misconceptions about women's capabilities as managers; (2) inhospitable informal structures; (3) recruitment, hiring, and promotion policies; and (4) perceived incompatibilities between career and family goals.

1. Misconceptions

Two kinds of misconceptions about women hamper their movement into management: biological-psychological misconceptions and socioeconomic misconceptions. As Jacklin and Maccoby indicate, the notion that women possess biological or psychological impediments or inferiorities that make it impossible for them to succeed in managerial positions is sheer myth. No significant differences between men and women have been found on such parameters as achievement motivation, intelligence, learning, sociability, or affiliation. The most important difference observed is that men are more aggressive than women. However, Jacklin and Maccoby emphasize that nothing in their findings correlates aggression with a willingness to tackle challenging assignments or to an ability to learn and exercise leadership skills. In short, there is no evidence to support the idea that women are less qualified psychologically for positions in management.

The stereotype of the emotional female is a particularly potent myth, an alleged handicap in assuming managerial responsibilities. Insel, in her comments on being the first woman manager in an organization, notes that at one of her jobs she faced what she regarded as a most peculiar proscription: "Never be emotional." She found this a difficult maxim because in her view, "we all (women and men) get emotional." Insel's observation finds scientific support in Jacklin and Maccoby's review. As they point out, both males and females can be "emotional." Both women and men have mood swings associated with hormonal cycles. And both women and men can be emotional toward others. As Jacklin and Maccoby report, "The male potential for empathetic and sympathetic emotional reactions, and the male potential for kindly, helpful behavior towards others (including children) seem to have been seriously underrated."

Another myth that hinders women's progress in management is that females are more unreliable because they tend to leave their jobs more frequently than men. This myth is laid to rest by Strober, who reports that where age and type of job are held constant, male-female turnover rates are about the same. Moreover, Strober's observation that "The female turnover rate can be reduced by any company that conscientiously seeks to do so" is substantiated repeatedly in the vignettes. Clearly, in families where the woman's career is important and the opportunity cost of her leaving the job is great, employment changes for both husband and wife receive careful consideration.

Scientific findings are important, but the positive experiences of women and their employers may be even more decisive in dispelling myths about women in management. We suggest that the problem of misinformation will be one of the more tractable ones in this field.

2. Inhospitable Informal Structures

Changing informal structures will undoubtedly be far more sticky. As Epstein points out in her chapter, the informal structures in most corporations are inhospitable to women. Austin gives personal testimony to this fact in her discussion of a summer work experience at a large New York–based company. Thoma, in her description of the questions she asks job interviewers, indicates that she is keenly aware not only of the usual unfriendly informal arrangements but also of their possible detrimental effects. "I realize that being excluded from situations where those informal rules enable access to the inside information . . . could reduce my ability to do my job well. And so I ask questions like, does Nancy go out to dinner with Harry and Bob?"

The rationale for many of the informal barriers facing women in management are described by Bradford, Sargent, and Sprague in their chapter on sexuality. They suggest that male sexuality is enhanced not only by executive power and status but also by the all-male exclusivity of the executive world. As a result, while most women managers view entry into informal groups simply in terms of work enhancement, the fact that matters of sexuality are involved for men makes inequality for women in this area one of the toughest to remedy. Other aspects of male-female interactions, along with concerns about actual or potential sexual attractions, are additional problems facing corporations and individuals.

Closely related to the issue of reforming informal structures is the extremely small number of women *now* in managerial positions. Insel, Austin, and Levine all comment upon the difficulties of the lone woman pioneer. In Insel's words, "being a pioneer woman is an exhausting task. I was hardly ever allowed to be tired. I was suspect when I was sick, I was generally expected to be perfect and was ready to defend myself at all times if I wasn't." And Levine explains, "It is very difficult to be first. Uncomfortable working environments are not unusual." Levine, Epstein, and Strober all point to the need to bring in more than one woman manager. Levine notes how difficult it is for a single woman to change an environment. Epstein writes, "It is essential to create a critical mass in management, a large enough proportion of women to make their presence a matter of course rather than a phenomenon." And Strober emphasizes that several women at the management level can encourage one another.

Avoiding tokenism may also help to alleviate problems that a sole woman manager sometimes finds in working with women who are *not* in managerial positions. Both Levine and Davey allude to the jealousies they have encountered on the part of nonmanagement women. A company that seeks to discover, encourage, and promote talent from within, one that is open to bringing large numbers of women into management, is probably less likely to have jealousy in the ranks than the company that opts for tokenism.

The problem of a very small number of women managers may well be transitory. In the 1960s women rarely chose management careers. Insel writes, "Many of my colleagues got law degrees, medical degrees; many more went to graduate school in the humanities and arts. I knew not one person who went to get a masters degree in business." And in Austin's words, "among my many friends who were considering graduate education, I did not know one who ever even mentioned . . . business school." Today, as Arjay Miller notes in the Introduction, female applicants to business schools are far more numerous. Not only are young women applying, but women like Blanchette are coming to business school to "retool." And equally significant are those women, like Davey and Pat Miller, who are seeking entry into management through nontraditional means. Women in the upper reaches of management are still rarities, but if women's socialization patterns do change, more young women will actively consider managerial careers and future female executives will rarely lack peers of their own sex. At that point some important changes in corporate informal interaction will undoubtedly be facilitated.

3. Present Recruitment, Hiring, and Promotion Policies

One of the key current problems for women management aspirants is the difficulty of "breaking through." As Epstein notes, women who have tried the secretary or gal Friday route have usually been disappointed. Women like Davey and Pat Miller who try to enter on the strength of their volunteer work records also find tremendous barriers. Even when in management positions, women are often rejected for promotion, as in the case "Perfectly Pure Peabody's."

Meacham, Strober, and Gordon all stress active involvement of executives in initiating successful programs for the recruitment, hiring, and promotion of women managers. The need to search widely for talented managers has been intensified by the very narrow judicial interpretation of the b.f.o.q. exception in Title IV of the Civil Rights Act and by the recent provisions in the Labor Department's Revised Order 4.[1] As noted, companies can demonstrate their commitment to increasing the number of women in management in many ways, including encouraging women applicants and employees, improving career counseling, revising recruiting procedures, altering job specifications, and increasing flexibility of job structures.

Will such changes be instituted by companies? We think they will be. The enthusiasm and success of current women managers, the awareness of the opportunity costs of not utilizing female talent, and the requirements and penalties of the law will all lead companies to try to institute effective policies. Of course, as has been noted several times in this volume, good intentions are a necessary but not sufficient ingredient for success. Companies will need to work intelligently at bringing women into management. As Gordon points out, they will need to put affirmative action on a par with other complex problems having a major impact. Top management's active commitment and willingness to reward and penalize managers for their actions in this field are two particularly important ingredients of a successful policy for bringing women into management.

4. Perceived Incompatibilities between Career and Family Goals

Women aspirants to business careers and many young businesswomen today represent a "new breed" of woman manager. Unlike their few female predecessors, these women are committed to twin goals: career *and* marriage. They are as unwilling to let a career rule out possibilities of marriage as they are to set aside career goals for those of home and hearth. This willingness to make two commitments is not unique to women contemplating or pursuing business careers. It has become the modus operandi for the majority of young professional women. Moreover, some women are making triple commitments: career, marriage, and children.

Multiple commitments can, of course, be immensely rewarding. Austin is pleased that she has not "gone the route of so many well-educated and reasonably talented women who could and should have had interesting careers of their own, but became discouraged somewhere along the line and transferred their hopes and aspirations to their husbands' careers." And Thoma and Levine both point out that marriages in which both husband and wife are pursuing careers can be very gratifying. As Thoma notes, given all the obstacles involved in coordinating two careers, it becomes "pretty obvious that the marriage is holding together because both parties want it to, not because it is the easy course to follow."

Yet the attempt to merge what, for women, once seemed to be two separate life-styles presents considerable difficulties. Thoma, Austin, and Levine all discuss the complexities experienced by dual career families. Deciding how to joint-maximize career interests is extremely delicate. Thoma says that she and her husband "tried a little of the decision science [we had] studied. . . . We each listed those cities where we felt our respective long-range job expectations could be met. After writing our cities by preference, we put our lists together and identified those cities that were acceptable to both of us." When Levine found her best job opportunity was in New York while her husband's was in Philadelphia, the couple "scribed arcs" and selected the halfway point as their residence. Later in their careers, when their best opportunities were geographically further apart, they set up a complicated commuting and living arrangement that included the inauguration of a second household.

Blanchette writes of some of the additional strains which

children can place on women's careers. Making complicated arrangements for the smooth functioning of a household with children requires considerable thought, time, energy, and emotion. Leisure time for mothers in professional or managerial positions is scarce indeed. Or, as Blanchette puts it, "I . . . sleep a great deal less than I did before."

Of the several knotty issues that surround the entry of women into management, the integration of career and family may prove the most challenging to individuals and to organizations. With the growing variations in life-styles, it promises to become an increasingly significant issue. Even male executives with nonworking spouses may begin to express greater interest in family-related goals.

B. NEW POSSIBILITIES

Any solutions to these problems will inevitably have an enormous impact on organizations. We believe that successful integration of women into management positions may have at least three major impacts on business: improved personnel practices, increased legitimacy of non-job-related goals, and a more widespread development of androgynous management styles.

1. Improved Personnel Practices

At the Stanford Women in Management Conference, the case "Perfectly Pure Peabody's" was discussed in several different workshops. In almost every group, a top executive remarked that certain aspects of Barrington's experience were also relevant for men, i.e., that, unfortunately, talented young male managers may also languish in organizations without being given appropriate encouragement, training, or exposure, and that the goals and aspirations of talented young male managers may also be inadequately communicated to or understood by their superiors.

As a result of legal requirements, and perhaps as a result of an awareness that women have been "overlooked" in the past, many employers are now beginning to examine somewhat more systematically the career goals of their female employees. In some instances, supervisors are beginning to offer women intel-

ligent suggestions for increased training and/or new job responsibilities. It is our belief that as the advantages to business of
improved career counseling become evident, there will be a
rather rapid spillover of benefits to male managers as they, too,
begin to find supervisors interested in their career goals and
aspirations.

Similar spillover benefits are likely to occur with respect to
recruitment policies. Strober has argued that women ought not
automatically be excluded from managerial training programs
simply because they are above a certain age. Obviously, the same
is true for men. Accelerated obsolescence of skills, the rapid
opening of new fields, and the secure knowledge that a wife's
income can provide basic family support during a husband's
training period will bring more and more men to seek "second
careers." Once business has found that it "pays" to train "older"
women they may also be willing to train "older" men. Similarly,
as it becomes commonplace to search for female managerial
talent in the volunteer sector or the educational sector, so too it is
likely to become accepted practice to search for talented male
executives in such heretofore-neglected fields as the arts and
journalism. Wider searches, accompanied by more enlightened
ideas about qualifications, will undoubtedly bring innovativeness
to the executive suite.

2. Increased Legitimacy of Non-Job-related Goals

The willingness of women managers to make commitments to
both family and career is also likely to have an important impact
on business organizations. Because bringing women into management is still in some sense an "experiment," those responsible
wish to be sure that no "damage" is done. Thus, many male
executives frequently become interested in the efforts of women
managers to integrate family and career goals. This interest may
be contagious. Once executives begin to be concerned about the
family-career adjustment of female managers, they may also
become aware of the adjustment of the male partners in dual-
career families. Eventually even the manager with a nonworking
wife may be perceived by the corporation as having legitimate
and important family-related goals. At the same time, as more and

more women managers successfully integrate career and family concerns, they may set an example. Male managers, observing that successful integration is indeed possible, may increasingly try transferring some of their own time and energies to family matters.

The possible effects of the increased legitimacy of family-related goals are great indeed: corporate willingness to experiment with part-time employment, paternal and maternal leave for child rearing, sabbatical leaves, postponement of travel-related training, and decreased penalties for an unwillingness to accept geographic transfer. But even more important, the legitimization of family-related goals in business may effect a legitimization of other non-job-related goals. Once it becomes acceptable for men and women to take a short leave for child rearing, it may also become acceptable to take a short leave to pursue a hobby or participate actively in a community project.

The opportunity for people to become multiple-goal-oriented would probably be tremendously healthy, for individuals and for society. As Bradford, Sargent, and Sprague note, men frequently define themselves in terms of their work; and women, traditionally, have defined themselves in terms of their husbands and children. But individuals whose identity is defined solely in terms of work or family often face serious problems. We are all familiar with the sense of tremendous deflation which many men experience upon retirement. We also know that a man who "peaks" in his productivity or creativity prior to retirement or a woman whose "nest" becomes empty often has feelings of inadequacy or uselessness. Seriously pursuing hobbies or self-development or community activities in addition to work and family throughout life can be important insurance against the possibility that work and/or family might at some time cease to be fully satisfying. At the same time, of course, these activities can add immensely to the richness of individuals' lives.

The effects on employee performance of widespread legitimization of non-job-related goals are, of course, unknown, and output may indeed be adversely affected by any dilution of attention to it. However, it is likely that productivity will not be so adversely affected. We believe that it is quite possible that job performance will be enhanced by a multiple-goal orientation; the old saw "All work and no play makes Jack a dull boy" may well have important implications for corporate creativity.

3. Development of Androgynous Management Styles

Many persons have speculated that bringing women into management will lead to the development of different management styles. For example, it is sometimes argued that since women have been socialized to be more "open" or "interpersonally aware," their management style is likely to be less autocratic than that of many men.

Much research is now taking place regarding differences in the ways in which men and women function as managers and as small-group participants. However, we believe that the primary impact of the entry of women into management will be less to add an alternative "feminine" management style than to hasten the development of an androgynous style of management.

"Androgyny" comes from the Greek words for man and woman. It refers to the blending of so-called masculine and feminine behaviors to produce a complete, well-balanced individual, unencumbered by sex-role prescriptions. Thus an androgynous management style would incorporate both so-called masculine styles and feminine styles. An androgynous manager might be both "aggressive" (that is, competitive, achievement-oriented, and determined) and also "open" (that is, able to understand subordinates' difficulties, willing to give honest criticism, and relatively amenable to revising goals).[2]

In discussions analyzing the implications of women's liberation, the concern is sometimes expressed that as women enter professional and managerial careers on an equal basis with men, they will lose the nurturant and empathetic feminine characteristics so highly valued for women by our society. Certainly such a development would be unfortunate. However, it is foreseeable that as women rise in status and power, so too will respect for stereotyped "female" characteristics. Perhaps then it will become acceptable and desirable for men, too, to adopt nurturant and empathetic behavior.

The development of androgynous management styles would

not mean that each individual would be "just like" every other. Nor would it mean the end to "la différence." Rather, it would allow men and women to incorporate individually the most effective and comfortable managerial characteristics without being overly concerned about whether those characteristics had been previously stereotyped as "male" or "female."

As the several authors in this volume emphasize, the problems of bringing women into management are manifold, and solutions are neither inexpensive nor facile. However, we are optimistic that solutions will emerge. Moreover, we regard attempts to bring women into management as well worth the effort, for if we succeed, we will have achieved not only an improvement in our utilization of human resources but also, quite possibly, an enhancement of our humanity.

NOTES

1 See U.S. Department of Labor, Office of Federal Contract Compliance, "Title 41—Public Contracts and Property Management, Chapter 60," *Federal Register*, vol. 36, no. 234, Dec. 4, 1971.

2 For further discussion of the concept of androgyny see S. L. Bem, "The Measurement of Psychological Androgyny," *Journal of Consulting and Clinical Psychology*, vol. 42, no. 2, 1974, pp. 155–162; and S. L. Bem, "Sex Role Adaptability: One Consequence of Psychological Androgyny," *Journal of Personality and Social Psychology*, forthcoming.

DUE DATE

MAY ~~APR~~ 1993			
~~APR 18~~			
MAY 25 1995			
~~OCT 18 2000~~			
			Printed in USA